Research in Human Development
Volume 2, Number 3

Special Issue: Successful Aging
Guest Editor: Susan Krauss Whitbourne

Successful Aging: Introductory Perspectives   99
Susan Krauss Whitbourne

What's So Good About Aging?   103
Robert L. Kane

An Attentional Perspective on Successful Socioemotional Aging:
Theory and Preliminary Evidence   115
Derek M. Isaacowitz

What Can We Learn From Longitudinal Studies
of Adult Development?   133
K. Warner Schaie

RESEARCH IN HUMAN DEVELOPMENT, 2(3), 99–102
Copyright © 2005, Lawrence Erlbaum Associates, Inc.

Successful Aging:
Introductory Perspectives

Susan Krauss Whitbourne
University of Massachusetts

Older adults are faced with numerous physical, psychological, and social role changes that challenge their sense of self and capacity to live happily. Nevertheless, the majority of older adults live fulfilling lives. The concept of successful aging was introduced to highlight the fact that growing older need not be synonymous with loss and decline (Rowe & Kahn, 1987, 1998). Although there are a number of possible definitions of *successful aging*, one that is perhaps the most inclusive incorporates three interactive components (Rowe & Kahn, 1998): absence of disease, maintenance of cognitive and physical functioning, and engagement with life. This definition takes into account the notion that there is a distinction to be made among primary (normal) aging, secondary (impaired), and optimal (successful) aging.

Within the field of human development, the study of successful aging provides an important challenge to the previously held assumption that childhood involves upward trajectories of growth and later adulthood involves an inevitable progression of decline. The notion of successful aging is also consistent with another principle in developmental science: Changes occur throughout life in a multidirectional, multidimensional fashion (Lerner, 1996). As is true in the early years of development, individuals in later life have the potential to increase, decrease, or remain stable within all areas of biological, psychological, and social functioning. Moreover, the potential for intervention exists throughout the years of later adulthood. Interventions can benefit older adults in areas ranging from physical functioning to emotional well-being. Such interventions can include exercise training to improve aerobic fitness, training in memory and fluid intelligence to reduce or offset cognitive decline, and psychotherapy to help individuals overcome depression and anxiety.

Requests for reprints should be sent to Susan Krauss Whitbourne, Department of Psychology, University of Massachusetts, Amherst, MA 01003. E-mail: swhitbo@psych.umass.edu

The study of human aging has maintained a focus not only on the potential for growth in the latter portion of the life span but also on the value of studying aging as a way to expand our knowledge about individuals of all ages. By learning about how individuals adapt to the challenges presented by the aging process, we gain an ability to appreciate concepts typically considered relevant to early life, such as vulnerability and resilience. Moreover, as developmental science increasingly moves toward a multidisciplinary approach, the study of aging represents the ideal paradigm for examining the interplay among biological, psychological, and social processes (Whitbourne, 2005).

With the graying of America and the world forecast to occur in the next 10 to 15 years, when over 20% of the population will be age 65 and older, it will be incumbent on the field of human development to include the study of aging as a vital part of the discipline. Not only will the incorporation of aging into the field enhance developmental science from a theoretical standpoint, but it will also have practical relevance. Professionals trained in the science and practice of human aging will be needed to provide vital services to the aging population, ranging from medical to psychosocial treatment. Moreover, as the Baby Boomer cohort moves from middle to later adulthood, new challenges will be presented both to practitioners and theoreticians. There is every reason to expect that this generation of older adults will, as they did throughout their lives, challenge the *establishment*. In this case, the establishment consists of the usual ways of defining and characterizing later life. By learning about what happens to the Baby Boomers as they move through the latter years of adulthood, developmental scientists will have a unique opportunity to understand and investigate the interaction between social context and individual patterns of development.

It has been a rewarding and welcome change to experience the expansion of the field of life-span development to include a truly integrative approach to the study of aging. Therefore, it was particularly encouraging to see the topic of successful aging included in the 2001 Biannual Meeting of the Society of the Study of Human Development. This issue of *Research on Human Development* includes three articles from that conference, each of which focuses on a different facet of the potential for growth and change in the later years of life.

In "What's So Good About Aging?," Robert L. Kane addresses head-on the issue of whether it is possible to age successfully given the numerous challenges presented by the aging process in the areas of primary aging, reflected in normative changes in bodily functioning, and by secondary aging, reflected in chronic diseases that become more prevalent with age. Kane presents what some might regard as a pessimistic view about aging, in that he reviews the biological, psychological, and social losses that occur in later life. He points out that prevention against primary and secondary aging can help to offset the losses associated with the aging process but that, by definition, aging is associated with decline in functioning. How is it, then, that older adults tend to have higher life satisfaction than younger adults? Have they developed special coping mechanisms? Kane argues that the key lies in the ability to make compromises and readjustments to changing life circumstances. Moreover, for those of us who are not yet old, we stand to learn from watching how these successful agers have managed to adapt so successfully to these challenges.

Moving on to psychosocial adjustment, Derek M. Isaacowitz, in his article "An Attentional Perspective on Successful Socioemotional Aging: Theory and Preliminary Evidence," examines the ways in which successful agers process information that has potentially negative implications. According to socioemotional selectivity theory (Carstensen, Isaacowitz, & Charles, 1999), as individuals reach major endings in their lives, they are able to regulate their affect so that they increase their experience of positive emotions and decrease their experience of negative emotions. Although such a process can occur at any point in the life span, clearly older individuals are more likely to be presented with an imminent ending. The theory's major proposition is that when faced with limited time, individuals are motivated to regulate their feelings as positively as possible. In a set of innovative experiments using eye-tracking measurements, Isaacowitz analyzed data on individual differences in personality and attention to negative information. Contrary to prediction, older adults with higher dispositional optimism scores spent longer amounts of time processing a negative stimulus. These findings suggest that perhaps older adults who age successfully have developed strong coping mechanisms that allow them to maintain a positive viewpoint when challenged by potentially threatening information. Thus, Kane and Isaacowitz are suggesting, on the basis of very different sources of data, that successful aging involves resilience in the face of adversity.

The final article by K. Warner Schaie, entitled "What Can We Learn From Longitudinal Studies of Adult Development?," echoes the themes of this volume in its emphasis on primary versus secondary aging, but it adds the vital dimension of the need to consider longitudinal data in studies on human development. Indeed, Schaie's sequential data set, known as the Seattle Longitudinal Study, has become the model on which subsequent researchers have based their efforts to tease apart ontogenetic from contextual influences. Cognitive aging is the specific topic on which the article focuses, but the points Schaie raises have applicability more generally to the study of developmental changes in later life.

The importance of approaching the aging process as an accumulation of both gains and losses is a major theme of Schaie's article. Throughout adulthood, individuals gain such qualities as wisdom and perspective, although, as he points out, the ability to benefit from experience is in part a function of personality and lifestyle. Flexibility and an ability to manage stress and conflict are attributes that can enhance an individual's ability to gain wisdom over the years of adulthood.

Schaie's analysis of the paradigms needed to examine change over time provides an excellent overview of the history of the field, and it should be considered mandatory reading for any course on longitudinal methodology. In addition to providing this background, Schaie summarizes contemporary approaches to the study of change. The very intriguing idea that age should be considered a dependent rather than an independent variable helps to provide further perspective on the problems faced by developmentalists who wish to examine change over significant portions of the life span.

Reinforcement of the importance of taking a biopsychosocial perspective is provided by Schaie's exploration of the possibility of using longitudinal data in the early detection of the risk of Alzheimer's disease. Testing individuals for the presence of a genetic marker that indicates heightened vulnerability to developing the disease and then following them longitudinally on cognitive performance is a method that could have both theoretical and applied value.

In summary, readers of this issue will be treated to an outstanding array of articles that cover a range of central issues in the study of successful aging. My hope is that this issue will serve as a stimulus to future research on aging that incorporates an integrative, biopsychosocial approach to the long-term study of change in the latter years of the life span. Moreover, each of these authors has provided a unique insight into the mystery and challenge that awaits us all: the ability to age successfully.

REFERENCES

Carstensen, L. L., Isaacowitz, D. M., & Charles, S. T. (1999). Taking time seriously: A theory of socioemotional selectivity. *American Psychologist, 54,* 165–181.

Lerner, R. M. (1996). Relative plasticity, integration, temporality, and diversity in human development: A developmental contextual perspective about theory, process, and method. *Developmental Psychology, 32,* 781–786.

Rowe, J. W., & Kahn, R. L. (1987). Human aging: Usual and successful. *Science, 237,* 143–149.

Rowe, J. W., & Kahn, R. L. (1998). *Successful aging.* New York: Pantheon Books.

Whitbourne, S. K. (2005). *Adult development and aging: Biopsychosocial perspectives* (2nd ed.). Hoboken, NJ: Wiley.

RESEARCH IN HUMAN DEVELOPMENT, 2(3), 103–114
Copyright © 2005, Lawrence Erlbaum Associates, Inc.

What's So Good About Aging?

Robert L. Kane

University of Minnesota School of Public Health

Despite the many claims by gerontologists that aging is an important and positive life experience, it is associated with many losses and much deterioration. Indeed, people seem to be willing to spend great sums in fruitless attempts to ward off its effects. On the other side, despite the many negative consequences of aging, many older persons seem quite content and able to cope well with its vicissitudes. We might do better not to celebrate the joys of aging but to admire the resilience of those who endure it.

"Aging is not for sissies" (multiple attributions)

"Aging is not so bad considering the alternatives" (multiple attributions)

We celebrate aging just like we admire most stories of survival. But surviving comes at a cost (R. Butler & Van Nostrand, 1975). Survival requires adaptation. Although one may genuinely celebrate becoming a centenarian, most of these people are struggling to ward off the impact of aging. Some are remarkably successful in maintaining their independence if not their health (Andersen-Ranberg, Schroll, Sci, & Jeune, 2001).

Although it is fashionable these days to emphasize the positive aspects of aging, realism demands that we acknowledge the pervasive negative features of aging. Anyone who ages, especially those who have achieved a full measure of seniority, can tell you that things get worse. Scientific studies confirm that organ system functions deteriorate with age (Sehl & Yates, 2001). Whether it is less energy and coordination or "senior moments," bad things occur more frequently with age. The abuses that a younger body could tolerate are not borne well by one that sags. Aging represents the accumulation of losses: loss of resiliency and responsiveness, loss of position, loss of friends and family, and loss of energy. In-

---

Requests for reprints should be sent to Robert L. Kane, University of Minnesota School of Public Health, Mayo Mail Code 197, 420 Delaware Street Southeast, Minneapolis, MN 55455. E-mail: kanex001@umn.edu

deed, the triumph of aging is the ability to cope with these losses and continue to lead a productive and fulfilling life.

The definition of what constitutes aging has changed. With advances in life expectancy among older people, the onset of old age has been revised upward, at least for some. However, the gains in longevity have not been altogether free of disability. Despite the demographic realities of aging for more years after age 65, society has been reluctant to change the chronological triggers for social programs like Medicare and Social Security, even when such steps make great financial and gerontological sense. For many, these programs represent rewards for having survived; for some, they are the prerequisite to survival.

Presumably everyone seeks to age well, but no one has officially determined just what constitutes successful aging (Phelan & Larson, 2002). The two most widely used descriptions come from large studies. Rowe and Kahn (1998) argued for the possibility of malleability even late in life. They included three components for successful aging: avoiding disease, engagement with life, and maintaining high physical and cognitive function. Although the emphasis is on preventive behaviors, several of these components allow a role for health care. Vaillant (2002) defined successful aging to include healthy aging, retirement, play and creativity, and generativity; the latter refers to a continual sense of intellectual and social development. Healthy aging includes objective physical disability, subjective physical health, length of undisabled life, objective mental health, objective social support, and subjective life satisfaction.

Successful aging is likely a combination of good genes, lifestyle, and luck. The challenge is to determine just how much is malleable. Some studies suggest that risk factors for adverse events like dementia may go way back to childhood (Danner, Snowdon, & Friesen, 2001; Snowdon et al., 1996). At the same time, it is hard to deny that things are improving overall. Survival at age 65 has increased. Although much of this new time has generally been spent in a condition of disability (especially for women), more recent estimates suggest at least modest gains in disability-adjusted life years.

We understand less about just why these improvements have come about. Much is likely attributable to overall improvements in living standards. Health promotion enthusiasts suggest that individual lifestyle changes can make a big difference. But what should one do? A whole generation grew up eating huge amounts of antioxidants in their Twinkies and Wonder Bread. Will they fare better? If junk food is bad for you, why start taking Vitamin E as an adult?

PREVENTION

Aging is not something we seek but accept as the consequence of advanced life expectancy. Many go not gently. The battle against aging is vividly reflected in contemporary advertising, in which a variety of products (from lotions to potions) promise to ward off either aging itself or the signs thereof. The existence of so much advertising suggests that many people are actively interested in joining the battle. Indeed the same baby boom generation that threatens the integrity of our social system when it ages seems to have taken the fight against aging as its own special crusade. This is not to suggest that earlier generations have not fought against aging by purchasing nostrums to ward off its ill effects. The current generation is pictured at least as also being willing to invest sweat equity (in exercise) in an effort to stave off the aging process.

The war against aging has become quite profitable. Some combatants are motivated by financial gain, whereas others see aging as a frontier for science. Both groups have been known to make extravagant claims (Binstock, 2003).

Some enthusiasts suggest that much of the decline associated with aging can be traced to preventable problems. If only we worked harder we could prevent these untoward events. In the scientific literature this phenomenon has come to be called the *compression of morbidity* (Fries, 1983). It holds that healthier living can prevent the onset of various problems that will affect the onset of morbidity and loss of function but will not influence the time of death. As a result, the period of life lived in a state of dependency will decrease. Ideally, old people under this scenario would live actively until they die suddenly.

We encourage people to fight the ravages of aging by prudent habits, believing that it is never too late to preserve and protect what we have left; but, just as with finances, it turns out that a lot depends on what we have brought to old age. Good bone mass, an active intellect, and a lifetime of exercise seem to raise the baseline from which deterioration can begin and, hence, slow the time until the level of decay crosses the threshold where bad things can be expected.

This realization has not dampened the enthusiasm for late-life rehabilitation. Exercise is widely touted as a remedy for various ills (Larson, 1991). Even persons in nursing homes are urged to exercise as much as possible to stave off decline (Fiatarone et al., 1994). However, the evidence to support such an aggressive approach to rehabilitation is not all that strong (Keysor & Jette, 2001). Based on an observation that high early intellectual performance seems to be a protective factor for dementia (S. M. Butler, Ashford, & Snowdon, 1996; Snowdon et al., 1996; Snowdon, Ostwald, & Kane, 1989), studies have been mounted to test the potential of introducing intellectual exercises for seniors to keep cognition strong (Ball et al., 2002). Here, too, more evidence about the efficacy of such a dramatic intervention is needed.

Proponents are quick to cite evidence that changing lifestyles can improve health, even at older ages (Fries, Bloch, Harrington, Richardson, & Beck, 1993; Fries, Koop, et al., 1993). There is some evidence from national surveys that the rate of age-specific disability is falling (Cutler, 2001; Manton, Corder, & Stallard, 1997; Manton & Gu, 2001), but the amount of decrease is modest. This view of aging is potentially optimistic, but it also contains echoes of an earlier era of preventive enthusiasm, which was paradoxically associated with blaming the victim (Knowles, 1977). In essence, if you are sick or disabled, you are responsible, because you failed to take the proper steps to prevent it. Old age is not thrust upon you; its ravages represent payback for failures of self-control or missed opportunities to take appropriately moderate steps in one's youth.

Some data suggest that it is possible to repent. Although primary prevention is best, preventing recurrences is also good. Active exercise and aspirin after a heart attack or a stroke seem to lower the risk of subsequent events (Awtry & Loscalzo, 2000; Dorn, Naughton, Imamura, & Trevisan, 1999; Hu et al., 2000; Sanmuganathan, Chahramani, Jackson, Wallis, & Ramsay, 2001; Vovko, Koudstaal, Bots, Hofman, & Breteler, 2001; Wannamethee & Shaper, 1999).

ILLNESS

The fight against aging is a major contributor to the growing costs of Medicare. Our standards for what can and should be treated have changed dramatically in the last decades. It is now common for 80-year-olds to have bypass surgery, for example. Whereas some urge rationing based on age (Callahan, 1987), many celebrate the end of ageism and the restriction of services on the basis of age (Wetle, 1987). Geriatrics champions eschew age as a criterion for eligibility and instead urge more functional criteria. Indeed, a strong argument can be made that age per se should not be the criterion for deciding if an expensive intervention should be implemented; but likelihood of survival—or, even better, likelihood of quality survival—does seem like a reasonable basis for rendering such a judgment. For some, even this approach is too restrictive (Avorn, 1984).

Perhaps the greatest challenge of geriatrics is to try to separate the effects of aging from those of disease. Decline in function is a concomitant of aging. Some argue that the decline is attributable to disease (e.g., heart output and heart disease; Geokas, Lakatta, Makinodan, & Timiras, 1990; Lakatta, 2000), but ignoring the effects of chronic illness is like looking at germ-free mice to get a view of normal living. Chronic disease is another concomitant of aging. It is obvious that chronic disease prevalence increases with age simply by virtue of accumulation.

The truth is that we live in an era of chronic disease. Perhaps a substantial proportion of that disease is attributable to our sloth and decadence (McGinnis & Foege, 1993), but it is a product of a lifestyle many value positively. Although we may flagellate ourselves for our imperfect behavior, it is also incumbent on the medical system to adjust its modus operandi to respond more effectively to the changing epidemiological reality of a predominance of chronic disease (Kane, 2000b).

LOSS OF INTELLECT

Perhaps the greatest scourge of aging is the loss of intellectual function. Although cognitive decline with age is not inevitable, the rising incidence of dementia with age makes the prospect grim. At least one study has estimated that by age 85 almost half (47.2%) of the population will have some degree of dementia (Evans et al., 1989), although others suggest that this rate is too high (Kawas, 2000). Longitudinal studies of cognitive performance suggest that decline is not inevitable (Schaie, 1990), but the incidence of dementia increases with age; by 85, the annual incidence is 8.4% (Hebert et al., 1995). There is some solace in the idea that we trade off different intellectual functions as we age to compensate for losses in one area (Baltes & Staudinger, 1993). Some believe the loss of intellect can be affected by actions akin to intellectual exercise (Ball et al., 2002; Wilson et al., 2002).

LOSSES AND ISOLATION

Social support is credited with much of the success behind successful aging (Rowe & Kahn, 1987, 1998). But, alas, aging is a time of loss. Not only do we lose function and reserve capacity, we lose friends and families. We lose social status. The older social gerontological theories of withdrawal have been supplanted by newer ideas of active engagement and changing roles (Marshall, 1999). However, it is hard to read the obituaries and not realize that older people lose dear ones at a brisk clip. Some may welcome retirement, but for others it marks a major loss of social role and self-definition. Leisure is fine until it becomes a burden to fill one's days. Moreover, leisure is expensive. It is one thing to retire wealthy and work actively on enjoyment. It is quite another to live on a fixed income and apportion expenses carefully.

For many people, especially men, one's social status is heavily determined by one's occupation. Work provides meaning for life. Certainly not all (or even most) people like their work. Nonetheless, it provides structure to their lives. Losing that structure can create a sense of loss along with the relief of getting rid of the stresses associated with the work.

Nonetheless older persons exhibit less diagnosable major depression than younger people (Koenig & Blazer, 1992). However, they do have a higher prevalence of depressive symptoms (not just somatic ones; Blazer, Burchett, Service, & George, 1991). These likely reflect a higher rate of medical illness and greater demands for caregiving.

INCOME

The diversity in functional aging is dwarfed by the variation in finances among older people. Old age happens to some of the wealthiest and the poorest in the land. Although the economic situation for older people has improved in aggregate, largely due to increases in Social Security such that age is no longer a pre-condition for poverty, African-American women age 85 and older are still among the poorest people in the land. In general, older women have less income than their male counterparts.

On the one hand, many older people bring substantial assets (usually a house) into retirement (79% of elder-headed households owned their home in 1997; 77% of these older homeowners owned their home free and clear). The median home value for elderly is $89,292 compared with $98,815 for the population overall. On the other hand, many older people face new expenses. Although persons age 65 and older are the only group in the United States to benefit from universal health insurance (Hayward, Shapiro, Freeman, & Corey, 1988), Medicare does not pay as much of the health costs as one might hope. A large proportion of older people's income goes toward health care. On average, older Medicare recipients paid $2,580 (or 19% of their income) for health care in 2000 (Brangan, 2001); but for poor people, the proportion is more like 30%. For many, a big cost is medications; but here too the distribution of burden varies greatly. Poor people (those below the poverty level) spend 9% of their income on medications, whereas the wealthy (those ≥400% above poverty level) spend only 2% (Gibson, Brangan, Gross, & Caplan, 1999).

STATUS AND POLITICAL POWER

In earlier times older people were thought to hold special status. Perhaps the mere fact of survival marked them as special. Perhaps their wisdom and knowledge were valued. Today, in an era of rapidly changing knowledge and revolving technology, lore is much less valued. The half-life for information is short; thus, experience is devalued. Indeed, familiarity with technology is prized.

Older people are often viewed as a powerful political force. Organizations like the American Association of Retired Persons (AARP) are seen as politically influential because of their large membership. However, studies show that older people rarely vote as a block (Binstock, 1997, 2000). Their lobbies are often effective at both the state and federal levels, largely because the potential of their political power is felt and their causes seem to be socially good. At the same time there has been a substantial political backlash. Images of "greedy geezers" and data suggesting that older people were in direct competition with children for social program dollars have made the elderly agenda considerably harder to sell.

LONG-TERM CARE

One of the most terrible negative signs of aging is the increased risk of long-term care (LTC). Age breeds frailty. The likelihood of entering a nursing home rises exponentially with age. The very fact that nursing homes exist seems to speak volumes about the political impotence of the aging lobby, but it is also a reflection of the inability of older constituents to accept the need for such services. Although large numbers of older people when polled emphatically state that they would rather be dead than in a nursing home (Mattimore et al., 1997), organizations like the AARP have never developed an effective political agenda to work toward the elimination of nursing homes and the establishment of a LTC system that more effectively meets older people's needs and aspirations. It is far from impossible to create an environment where frail older people can live as residents and still enjoy high levels of autonomy while receiving the services they need.

However, LTC has never been a politically attractive topic. No politician has been willing to make it an active part of his or her platform. Efforts to place the issue on the political agenda have been notoriously unsuccessful. The reason for this failure is unclear. One real possibility is that no one believes the problem can be solved, at least not without investing huge sums of money. People are reluctant to make a large investment because they do not believe that care makes much of a difference (Kane, 2000a). LTC seems to be viewed as a necessary social service but not necessarily one that makes a difference in physiological outcomes or quality of life. Obviously some sort of care must be given to respond to identified needs, but the type and amount does not seem to matter. Hence, it is an unenthusiastic investment, especially compared to the prevalent mythology about the value of medical interventions. Ironically, good LTC does make a difference. It can both slow the rate of functional decline (largely by eliminating iatrogenic problems) and improve people's quality of life.

END-OF-LIFE CARE

Gerontologists count backwards from death in determining age. For them age reflects the probability of dying. It is hardly surprising that many geriatricians have become actively involved in end-of-life care. This palliative care approach, which traces its origins to the hospice movement (Saunders, 1978), argues for a transfer of effort from sustaining life to making the end of life more comfortable (SUPPORT Principal Investigators, 1995). A related effort, which has been sold as a means to increase patient autonomy, is the active use of advance directives. The focus here is on determining (and adhering to) the preferences for or against life-sustaining treatment for persons who have lost the capacity to speak for themselves. Ignoring the irony of pressing for autonomy for the comatose while ignoring the preferences of the alert, this philosophy requires people to define and codify their preferences for hypothetical situations of greatly limited function. Unfortunately, most people are inclined to underestimate greatly the value of life under such circumstances (Sackett & Torrance, 1978). Hence, they are abrogating their rights to care that they might actually want if they had the opportunity to ask for it (Danis, Patrick, Southerland, & Green, 1988; Tsevat et al., 1998). Advance directives need to be carefully distinguished from end-of-life decisions on two grounds: (a) The former are based on hypothetical utility weights about how someone might value living in a given state that has never been experienced, and (b) the latter are made by people actually experiencing the condition at the time of the decision making or close to that time.

Some see in the advance directives advocacy a cruel plot to move toward a form of rationing by duplicitously preying on those least able to protect themselves and doing it under the banner of enhancing autonomy. Older people are undoubtedly major consumers of health care, and caring for them can be costly. Because they use well beyond their proportionate share of health resources, they are prime targets for rationing. Their candidacy is enhanced by society's generally negative views about the value of old age. Some have been willing to confront the issue directly, arguing that older people have a moral imperative to pass opportunities for life's experiences to the young (Callahan, 1987). More often the arguments are convoluted, although the message is the same.

Even in the absence of strong social programs, some age-based rationing seems to be occurring. For example, medical care in the last year of life is less intense for older people (Levinsky et al., 2001). Indeed, the intensiveness of medical care in general decreases with age. It is not clear if this reflects ageism, or if survivors are a hardier lot (Lubitz, Beebe, & Baker, 1995).

THE PARADOX

The great unanswered marvelous question remains: If aging is associated with all these bad events, why aren't older people more unhappy? It is probably not enough to suggest that they are satisfied simply to have survived. They report higher life satisfaction than their younger counterparts. Something else seems to be in play. For gerontologists aging is measured less by chronological years than by the force of mortality, the risk of death. Older persons must surely be more aware of their imminent mortality, but they appear to have developed strong coping mechanisms. Perhaps the awareness of the finitude of life motivates people to get more out of it.

A wide variety of coping mechanisms have been postulated. Baltes and Baltes (1990) proposed a theory of selective optimization with compensation whereby older people focus on areas in which they can perform best. Another theory posits that older people make temporal comparisons of themselves to their peers and generally come away feeling positive (Rosenberg, 1979). Some suggest that older persons simply avoid problems and accept difficulties they cannot avoid (Aldwin, Sutton, Chaira, & Spiro, 1996). Other variants talk about assimilative and adaptive coping (Brandstadter & Greve, 1994), shifting the mechanisms of control

(Heckhausen & Schultz, 1995), or revising one's sense of self (Herzog & Markus, 1999; Sneed, 2003).

All of these coping mechanisms have in common the underlying sense of loss and worsening status and some means of withdrawal or retrenchment. Ironically, these concepts of withdrawal and isolation were precisely the theories of aging that were rejected in favor of a more optimistic view several decades ago (Marshall, 1999). It appears we have come full circle without acknowledging the orbit.

We are left with hollow advice about how to achieve mental health in old age:

- Maintain mastery in dealing with issues of life.
- Achieve congruence between aspirations and achievement.
- Derive pleasure from life's activities.
- Sustain an optimistic outlook (Gatz & Zarit, 1999).

These sorts of coping strategies reflect a view that much has been lost with age and older people must work hard to maintain what they have, even to the point of readjusting their aspirations and perhaps their grasp on reality.

CONCLUSION

We had better get good at aging because more people are doing it. Aging is tough. It is associated with losses in various areas, but some people seem to have a knack for dealing with it. The fact that some people can maintain their positive attitudes and even a fair amount of their physical vigor in the face of the considerable negative effects of aging is something to marvel at, but it does not detract from the reality that aging is essentially a time of loss. The answer is not to deny the fact of these declines or to continue to seek notions and potions to ward off the ravages of aging (although we inevitably will) but rather to recognize the effects of aging and celebrate (and learn from) those who have risen to the challenge aging poses. Successful aging involves a lot of coping. Coping involves a lot of compromises and readjustments.

So, what is so good about aging? The very fact of survival is usually something to celebrate given the alternative. For a lucky few that survival comes with only modest costs, but aging takes its toll on most of us. Most seem willing to pay the price, but all secretly or overtly yearn to find a magic way to avoid the negative concomitants of aging.

REFERENCES

Aldwin, C. M., Sutton, K. J., Chaira, G., & Spiro, A. (1996). Age differences in stress, coping and appraisal: Findings from the Normative Aging Study. *Journal of Gerontology: Psychological Sciences, 51B*, P179–P188.

Andersen-Ranberg, K., Schroll, M., Sci, M., & Jeune, B. (2001). Healthy centenarians do not exist, but autonomous centenarians do: A population-based study of morbidity among Danish centenarians. *Journal of the American Geriatrics Society, 49*(7), 900–908.

Avorn, J. (1984). Benefit and cost analysis in geriatric care: Turning age discrimination into health policy. *New England Journal of Medicine, 310*(20), 1294–1301.

Awtry, E. H., & Loscalzo, J. (2000). Aspirin. *Circulation, 101*(10), 1206–1218.

Ball, K., Berch, D. B., Helmers, K. F., Jobe, J. B., Leveck, M. D., Marsiske, M., Morris, J. N., et al. (2002). Effects of cognitive training interventions with older adults: A randomized controlled trial. *Journal of the American Medical Association, 288*(18), 2271–2281.

Baltes, P., & Baltes, M. (Eds.). (1990). *Successful aging: Perspectives from the behavioral sciences.* Cambridge, England: Cambridge University Press.

Baltes, P., & Staudinger, U. (1993). The search for psychology of wisdom. *Current Directions in Psychological Science, 2*, 75–80.

Binstock, R. H. (1997). The 1996 election: Older voters and implications for policies on aging. *The Gerontologist. 37*(1), 15–19.

Binstock, R. H. (2000). Older people and voting participation: Past and future. *The Gerontologist, 40*(1), 18–31.

Binstock, R. H. (2003). The war on "anti-aging medicine." *The Gerontologist, 43*(1), 4–14.

Blazer, D., Burchett, B., Service, C., & George, L. K. (1991). The association of age and depression among the elderly: An epidemiologic exploration. *Journal of Gerontology: Medical Sciences, 46*, M210–M215.

Brandstadter, J., & Greve, W. (1994). The aging self: Stabilizing and protective processes. *Developmental Review, 14*, 52–80.

Brangan, N. (2001). *AARP data digest.* Washington, DC: Public Policy Institute, American Association of Retired Persons.

Butler, R., & Van Nostrand, J. (1975). *Why survive? Being old in America.* New York: Harper & Row.

Butler, S. M., Ashford, J. W., & Snowdon, D. A. (1996). Age, education, and changes in the Mini Mental State Exam scores of elderly women: Findings from the nun study. *Journal of the American Geriatrics Society, 44*, 675–681.

Callahan, D. (1987). *Setting limits: Medical goals in an aging society.* New York: Simon & Schuster.

Cutler, D. M. (2001). Declining disability among the elderly. *Health Affairs, 20*(6), 11–27.

Danis, M., Patrick, D. L., Southerland, L. I., & Green, M. L. (1988). Patients' and families' preferences for medical intensive care. *Journal of the American Medical Association, 260*, 797–802.

Danner, D., Snowdon, D., & Friesen, W. (2001). Positive emotions in early life and longevity: Findings from the nun study. *Journal of Personality and Social Psychology, 80*(5), 804–813.

Dorn, J., Naughton, J., Imamura, D., & Trevisan, M. (1999). Results of a multicenter randomized clinical trial of exercise and long-term survival in myocardial infarction patients: The National Exercise and Heart Disease Project (NEHDP). *Circulation, 100*(17), 1764–1769.

Evans, D., Funkenstein, H., Albert, M., Scherr, P., Cook, N., Chown, M., Hebert, L., et al. (1989). Prevalence of Alzheimer's disease in a community population of older persons: Higher than previously reported. *Journal of the American Medical Association, 262*(18), 2551–2556.

Fiatarone, M. A., O'Neill, E. F., Ryan, N. D., Clements, K. M., Solares, G. R., Nelson, M. E., Roberts, S. B., et al. (1994). Exercise training and nutritional supplementation for physical frailty in very elderly people. *New England Journal of Medicine, 330*(25), 1769–1775.

Fries, J. F. (1983). The compression of morbidity. *Milbank Memorial Fund Quarterly, 61*, 397–419.

Fries, J. F., Bloch, D. A., Harrington, H., Richardson, N., & Beck, R. (1993). Two-year results of a randomized controlled trial of a health promotion program in a retiree population: The Bank of America study. *The American Journal of Medicine, 94*, 455–462.

Fries, J. F., Koop, C. E., Beadle, C. E., Cooper, P. P., England, M. J., Greaves, R. F., Sokolov, J. J., et al. (1993). Reducing health care costs by reducing the need and demand for medical services. *The New England Journal of Medicine, 329*(5), 321–325.

Gatz, M., & Zarit, S. H. (1999). A good old age: Paradox or possibility. In V. L. Bengtson & K. W. Schaie (Eds.), *Handbook of theories of aging* (pp. 396–416). New York: Springer.

Geokas, M. C., Lakatta, E. G., Makinodan, T., & Timiras, P. S. (1990). The aging process. *Annals of Internal Medicine, 113*(6), 455–466.

Gibson, M. J., Brangan, N., Gross, D., & Caplan, C. (1999). *How much are Medicare beneficiaries paying out-of-pocket for prescription drugs?* Washington, DC: American Association of Retired Persons Public Policy Institute.

Hayward, R. A., Shapiro, M. F., Freeman, H. E., & Corey, C. R. (1988). Inequities in health services among insured Americans: Do working-age adults have less access to medical care than the elderly? *New England Journal of Medicine, 318*, 1507–1511.

Hebert, L. E., Scherr, P. A., Beckett, L. A., Albert, M. S., Pilgrim, D. M., Chown, M. J., Funkenstein, H. H., et al. (1995). Age-specific incidence of Alzheimer's disease in a community population. *Journal of the American Medical Association, 273*(17), 1354–1359.

Heckhausen, J., & Schultz, R. (1995). A life-span theory of control. *Psychological Review, 102*, 284–304.

Herzog, A. R., & Markus, H. R. (1999). The self-concept in life span and aging research. In V. L. Bengtson & K. W. Schaie (Eds.), *Handbook of theories of aging* (pp. 227–252). New York: Springer.

Hu, F. B., Stampfer, M. J., Colditz, G. A., Ascherio, A., Rexrode, K. M., Willett, W. C., & Manson, J. E. (2000). Physical activity and risk of stroke in women. *Journal of the American Medical Association, 283*(22), 2961–2967.

Kane, R. L. (2000a). Changing the image of long-term care. *Age and Ageing, 29*, 481–483.

Kane, R. L. (2000b). The chronic care paradox. *Journal of Aging & Social Policy, 11*(2/3), 107–114.

Kawas, C., Gray, S., Brookmeyer, R., Fozard, J., & Zonderman, A. (2000). Age-specific incidence rates of Alzheimer's disease: The Baltimore Longitudinal Study of Aging. *Neurology, 54*(11), 2072–2077.

Keysor, J. J., & Jette, A. M. (2001). Have we oversold the benefit of late-life exercise? *Journal of Gerontology: Medical Sciences, 56A*(7), M412–M423.

Knowles, J. (1977). Responsibility of the individual. In J. Knowles (Ed.), *Doing better and feeling worse* (pp. 57–80). New York: Norton.

Koenig, H. G., & Blazer, D. G. (1992). Mood disorders and suicide. In J. E. Birren, R. B. Sloane, N. R. Cohen, B. D. Hooyman, M. Lebowitz, M. Wykle, & D. E. Deutchman (Eds.), *Handbook of mental health and aging* (2nd ed., pp. 380–400). New York: Academic.

Lakatta, E. G. (2000). Cardiovascular aging in health. *Clinics in Geriatric Medicine, 16*(3), 419–444.

Larson, E. B. (1991). Exercise, functional decline, and frailty. *Journal of the American Geriatrics Society, 39*(6), 635–636.

Levinsky, N., Yu, W., Ash, A., Moskowitz, M., Gazelle, G., Saynina, O., & Emanuel, E. (2001). Influence of age on medical expenditures and medical care in the last year of life. *Journal of the American Medical Association, 286*(11), 1349–1355.

Lubitz, J., Beebe, J., & Baker, C. (1995). Longevity and Medicare expenditures. *The New England Journal of Medicine, 332*(15), 999–1003.

Manton, K. G., Corder, L., & Stallard, L. (1997). Chronic disability trends in elderly United States populations: 1982–1994. *Medical Sciences, 94*, 2593–2598.

Manton, K. G., & Gu, X. (2001). Changes in the prevalence of chronic disability in the United States black and nonblack population above age 65 from 1982 to 1999. *Proceedings of the National Academy of Sciences, 98*(11), 6354–6359. Retrieved 1 August 2004 from www.pnas.org/cgi/doi/6310.1073/pnas.111152298

Marshall, V. W. (1999). Analyzing social theories of aging. In V. L. Bengtson & K. W. Schaie (Eds.), *Handbook of theories of aging* (pp. 434–455). New York: Springer.

Mattimore, T. J., Wenger, N. S., Cesbiens, N. A., Teno, J. M., Hamel, M. B., Liu, H., Carliff, R., et al. (1997). Surrogate and physician understanding of patients' preferences for living permanently in a nursing home. *Journal of the American Geriatrics Society, 45*, 818–824.

McGinnis, J. M., & Foege, W. H. (1993). Actual causes of death in the United States. *Journal of the American Medical Association, 270*(18), 2207–2212.

Phelan, E. A., & Larson, E. B. (2002). Successful aging—where next? *Journal of the American Geriatrics Society, 50*(7), 1306–1308.

Rosenberg, M. (1979). *Conceiving the self.* New York: Basic Books.

Rowe, J. W., & Kahn, R. L. (1987). Human aging: Usual and successful. *Science, 237*, 143–149.

Rowe, J. W., & Kahn, R. L. (1998). *Successful aging.* New York: Random House.

Sackett, D. L., & Torrance, G. W. (1978). The utility of different health states as perceived by the general public. *Journal of Chronic Diseases. 31*, 697–704.

Sanmuganathan, P. S., Chahramani, P., Jackson, P. R., Wallis, E. J., & Ramsay, L. E. (2001). Aspirin for primary prevention of coronary heart disease: Safety and absolute benefit related to coronary risk derived from meta-analysis of randomised trials. *Heart, 85*(3), 265–271.

Saunders, C. (1978). Hospice care. *American Journal of Medicine, 65*, 726–728.

Schaie, K. W. (1990). The optimization of cognitive functioning in old age: Predictions based on cohort-sequential and longitudinal data. In P. B. Baltes & M. M. Baltes (Eds.), *Successful aging: Perspectives from the behavioral sciences* (pp. 94–117). Cambridge, England: Cambridge University Press.

Sehl, M. E., & Yates, F. E. (2001). Kinetics of human aging I: Rates of senescence between ages 30 and 70 years in healthy people. *Journal of Gerontology: Biological Sciences, 56A*(5), B198–B208.

Sneed, J. R., & Whitbourne, S. K. (2003). Identity processing and self-consciousness in middle and later adulthood. *Journals of Gerontology Series B—Psychological Sciences & Social Sciences. 58*(6), 313–319.

Snowdon, D. A., Kemper, S. J., Mortimer, J. A., Greiner, L. H., Wekstein, D. R., & Markesbery, W. R. (1996). Linguistic ability in early life and cognitive function and Alzheimer's disease in late life: Findings from the nun study. *Journal of the American Medical Association. 275*(7), 528–532.

Snowdon, D. A., Ostwald, S. K., & Kane, R. L. (1989). Education, survival, and independence in elderly Catholic sisters, 1936–1988. *American Journal of Epidemiology, 130*, 999–1012.

SUPPORT Principal Investigators. (1995). A controlled trial to improve care for seriously ill hospitalized patients: The study to understand prognoses and preferences for outcomes and risks of treatments (SUPPORT). *Journal of the American Medical Association, 274*(20), 1591–1598.

Tsevat, J., Dawson, N. V., Wu, A. W., Lynn, J., Soukup, J. R., Cook, E. F., Vidaillet, H., et al. (1998). Health values of hospitalized patients 80 years or older: HELP investigators. Hospitalized Elderly Longitudinal Project. *Journal of the American Medical Association, 279*(5), 371–375.

Vaillant, G. E. (2002). *Aging well: Surprising guideposts to a happier life from the Landmark Harvard Study of Adult Development.* Boston: Little, Brown.

Vovko, Z., Koudstaal, P. J., Bots, M. L., Hofman, A., & Breteler, M. M. (2001). Aspirin use and risk of stroke in the elderly: The Rotterdam Study. *Neuroepidemiology, 20*(1), 40–44.

Wannamethee, S. G., & Shaper, A. G. (1999). Physical activity and the prevention of stroke. *Journal of Cardiovascular Risk, 6*(4), 213–216.

Wetle, T. (1987). Age as a risk factor for inadequate treatment. *Journal of the American Medical Association. 258*, 516.

Wilson, R. S., Mendes de Leon, C. F., Barnes, L. L., Schneider, J. A., Bienias, J. L., Evans, D. A., & Bennett, D. A. (2002). Participation in cognitively stimulating activities and risk of incident Alzheimer's disease. *Journal of the American Medical Association, 287*, 742–748.

RESEARCH IN HUMAN DEVELOPMENT, 2(3), 115–132

An Attentional Perspective on Successful Socioemotional Aging: Theory and Preliminary Evidence

Derek M. Isaacowitz

Brandeis University

What are the information-processing mechanisms that underlie successful affect regulation across the life span? Recent evidence suggests a rather positive view of affect regulation into late life, and socioemotional selectivity theory has been proposed as a motivational account that may help explain these findings. In particular, the theory argues that emotions and their regulation become more salient as people age. After reviewing recent evidence primarily concerning emotional memory in late life, a theoretical rationale is presented for investigating the role of attention to emotional stimuli as a mechanism for understanding successful affect regulation across the adult life span. Then, a program of research using eye tracking to study these attentional processes is described, and initial results are presented suggesting that there may be both age and individual difference effects on attention to emotional stimuli in adulthood.

The recent news from the field of socioemotional aging is positive, maybe even surprisingly so. As more and more evidence has emerged pointing to impressive affective resilience as people age, the search has begun for the psychological mechanisms underlying this resilience, particularly given the well-documented negative effects of aging on many aspects of health and cognitive functioning (Whitbourne, 2005). In this article, I review the recent evidence suggesting this optimistic picture of affect in late life and then discuss how researchers have attempted to understand these normative age effects by investigating the role of information processing in socioemotional aging. The remainder of the article focuses on an approach I have been developing to try to isolate and better understand the role cognition plays in well-being using eye-tracking methodology. In

Requests for reprints should be sent to Derek M. Isaacowitz, Department of Psychology, Brandeis University, MS 062, Waltham, MA 02454–9110. E-mail: dmi@brandeis.edu addition to presenting a rationale and description for this approach, I also review data we have collected so far, as well as theoretical speculations concerning what these results mean and how best to proceed toward a better understanding of the underlying mechanisms involved.

AFFECT AND AGING: AN EMERGING PICTURE

Despite early theoretical speculation that affective life may dampen with age (e.g., Schulz, 1985), the actual advent of empirical research on age differences in affect have led to a very different set of conclusions. First, several studies comparing self-reported affect of young and old adults found a good deal of similarity between groups (Malatesta & Kalnok, 1984) and some differences suggesting better emotional control by older individuals (Gross et al., 1997; Lawton, Kleban, Rajagopal, & Dean, 1992). More recent self-report affect data from the large National Survey of Midlife Development in the United States (MIDUS) sample of adults aged 25 to 75 suggested that older adults reported higher levels of positive affect and lower levels of negative affect than their younger counterparts (Mroczek & Kolarz, 1998). However, a similar study using data from the Berlin Aging Study of individuals aged 70 to 100 found no unique age effects on either positive or negative affect in this older sample (Isaacowitz & Smith, 2003).

Other studies have gone beyond simple, one-time, cross-sectional, self-report investigations to understand age effects on affect. For example, Carstensen, Pasupathi, Mayr, and Nesselroade (2000) conducted an experience-sampling study in which adults aged 18 to 94 were beeped five times a day for 7 days and reported on their current affective state at each beep. No age differences emerged for intensity of positive or negative affect or for frequency of positive affect. Negative affect appeared to be less frequent with age but only up to age 60, after which there was a slight upswing. More recently, Charles, Reynolds, and Gatz (2001) used the rich cohort-sequential data from the University of Southern California (USC) Generations Study to test for both age and cohort effects on affect in adulthood. Negative affect again appeared to decline until about age 60, although individuals high in Neuroticism did not show this age-related improvement in affect. Thus, although the news on affective aging is not endlessly positive, it is indeed quite optimistic, especially given the negative trajectories taking place simultaneously in other domains.

Socioemotional selectivity theory (Carstensen, Isaacowitz, & Charles, 1999) has been offered as a motivational account of why the emotional trajectory may be as positive as it is across the adult life span. According to the theory, individuals' time orientation has critical effects on their motivation; when time is perceived as open ended, individuals are motivated to pursue goals that will benefit them in their relatively expansive future, regardless of the ramifications of that goal pursuit for how they feel. In contrast, the theory proposes that individuals who perceive their time as more limited will be motivated to pursue goals that will benefit them in the present rather than in the uncertain future. In particular, goals of feeling good and of emotion regulation have this feature (Carstensen, 1993). Thus, perceiving time as limited should be associated with motivation to pursue affectively rewarding goals. Although the actual experience of affect in the face of limited time may not be unabashedly positive given the possibility of poignant mixed emotions as individuals face endings (Carstensen et al., 2000), the theory claims that the underlying motivation in the face of limited time is to regulate feelings in the most positive possible way.

The theory originated in the study of social gerontology to explain the finding that older individuals appear to focus on closest socioemotional partners and eliminate acquaintances from their social networks (Carstensen, 1992; Lang, Staudinger, & Carstensen, 1998). However, the idea that older individuals are focused more on emotional goals than their younger counterparts was easily applied to understanding why affective trajectories are so positive in late life. The theory argues that older individuals are leading rewarding affective lives because they are motivated to focus on emotion regulation in their social choices and more general goal pursuit. In other words, older adults may be motivated to work on their emotions; they are happy because being happy is important to them, and they are proactively working to achieve good affective states.

Note that advancing age is not the only context in which affective goals become prioritized. Other contexts in which time is perceived as limited, such as the turnover of Hong Kong from Britain to China (Fung, Carstensen, & Lutz, 1999) and terminal illness (Carstensen & Fredrickson, 1998), have been shown to lead to a focus on emotion in a similar manner as age. Thus, the phenomenon of limited time perspective leading to a motivated focus on emotional goals is not unique to late life, but rather it is a more general process. Whenever time is perceived as limited, emotions become more salient to individuals, regardless of age (Carstensen et al., 1999). As Carstensen and Turk-Charles (1994) put it, age may be one case of a context in which there is "an overall shift in cognitive operations such that emotions become increasingly salient" (p. 263).

SOCIOEMOTIONAL SELECTIVITY IN INFORMATION PROCESSING: WHERE IS IT?

An obvious question emerging from the theory and research just described is as follows: What are the psychological properties of this salience conceptualized to be a core feature of socioemotional aging? When vision researchers discuss salience, they tend to mean properties of a stimulus that make it particularly attention grabbing, such as color or contour (Parkhurst, Law, & Niebur, 2002).

However, salience in socioemotional selectivity terms is more about psychological aspects of the environment that match motivated goals of an individual. The implication is that, at some point in the processing of information from the world, some information gets preferred processing because it corresponds to motivated goals of the processor. But where in the processing of stimuli from the environment does this match of stimulus to motivation take place? Put another way, when during information processing does this salience of emotion actually impact how the environment is cognitively engaged? How is it that some individuals end up focused on aspects of their environment that promote emotion regulation and others focus on different aspects of the environment, such as those that would promote accurate memory?

Early research on the role of emotional salience on information processing across the life span focused on memory as the site of such effects. In the first study on cognition and socioemotional selectivity, Carstensen and Turk-Charles (1994) found no overall age effects on an incidental text recall task, but instead they found age differences in the content of what was remembered. Whereas younger participants recalled more of the factual aspects of the text, older participants remembered more of the affective and subjective content. This finding was consistent with research emerging from several groups studying cognitive aging suggesting that older adults' source memory was focused on affect (Hashtroudi, Johnson, Vnek, & Ferguson, 1994) and that recollection of personal events was more subjective and less factual in older as compared to younger couples (Gould & Dixon, 1993; see Isaacowitz, Charles, & Carstensen, 2000, for a more thorough review).

More recently, several studies have identified age differences in memory for emotional stimuli that might suggest that the salience of socioemotional selectivity primarily acts on memory to produce age differences in how emotional material is remembered. Fung and Carstensen (2003) showed that emotional messages are better remembered by older individuals than are nonemotional ones. Charles, Mather, and Carstensen (2003) used emotional images and found that older individuals showed a unique forgetfulness for negative but not positive images. Young adults showed no such forgetfulness. Kennedy, Mather, and Carstensen (in press) found a similar positive bias in older adults' memory for personal events.

IS MEMORY THE ANSWER?

These studies provide a compelling case for the salience of emotion being a memory issue. But there are several critical reasons why aspects of information processing that unfold before memory should also be considered as possible sites of the emotional salience effect that comes with age. Most simply, memory is itself a result of a number of earlier cognitive operations, such as attention, that may impact what is to be remembered (see, e.g., Cowan, 1988; Revelle, 1993). Although it is not entirely impossible to show some memory for stimuli that were not attended, it certainly does not help (Wood, Stadler, & Cowan, 1997); in other words, it would be logical to think that what is most attended to is also the information from the environment that is most encoded into memory and best recalled later.

There are a number of reasons to regard attention as the most interesting cognitive operation when investigating how emotional salience impacts information processing. First, attention is the most selective stage of information processing. During the attentional stage, the largest amount of possible material is weaned down to the smallest amount possible to facilitate efficient processing. Second, perspectives such as chaos theory (see, e.g., Masterpaqua & Perna, 1997) remind us that very small differences in initial conditions can lead to exponentially large differences in output. Given the sizable differences in behavioral outcome (what is remembered, what goals are pursued, etc.) in the studies just reviewed, understanding the causes of those differences may benefit from a consideration of the earliest aspects of processing at which they may diverge. This is not memory, but instead it involves processes surrounding attention. When differences between groups are found relatively late in information processing, it is still critical to investigate possible divergences relatively early in information processing. This point is one well appreciated by experimental psychopathology researchers in particular; in their attempts to understand the cognitive processes that underlie and maintain clinical phenomena like anxiety, they have focused on attention as a stage at which the information processed by anxious individuals may differ from that processed by nonanxious individuals (see, e.g., Mogg & Marden, 1990). Indeed, anxious individuals do appear to show attentional biases such that they favor threatening stimuli in ways not seen in nonanxious individuals (see J. M. G. Williams, Watts, MacLeod, & Matthews, 1997).

What, then, do we make of attention in socioemotional selectivity theory's account of how emotion becomes more salient with age? I believe that it is no accident that older individuals are said to focus more on emotion in some versions of the theory; for example, in the concluding comments to Carstensen et al. (1999), we argued that "the approach of endings is related to . . . increased focus on emotion regulation in everyday life" (p. 178). For this reason, and the ones already described, it seems both logical and important to consider the possibility that the action in socioemotional selectivity appears predominantly in attentional processes. In the aforementioned Charles et al. (2003) study in which older adults seemed to forget negative images, some basic looking time data (i.e., the amount of time until they clicked off a particular image) suggested that participants of all ages actually looked more at the negative images, making the older adults' forgetting them all the more impressive. In a separate study using a dot-probe design in which participants pressed a button when a probe appeared following an emotional face, older participants were faster to respond to probes following neutral faces when they were paired with negative ones (Mather & Carstensen, 2003). Faster latencies on this task indicate attentional preference or bias (J. M. G. Williams et al., 1997), so the findings suggest that older adults were orienting their attention away from the negative faces.

Recently, researchers in experimental psychopathology have attempted to transcend the constraints implicit in attention tasks like the dot-probe (e.g., not being able to distinguish attentional biases from response biases; Mogg, Millar, & Bradley, 2000) through methodologies that directly measure attention to visually presented stimuli. Eye tracking allows for just such measurement, as gaze generally is identical to attention (Parkhurst, Law, & Niebur, 2002). Therefore, I have decided to pursue a program of research in my lab using eye tracking as a tool for understanding exactly how information processing underlies age differences in affect and affect regulation.

EYE-TRACKING STUDIES OF AGING AND ATTENTION TO EMOTIONAL STIMULI

In my lab, we have completed one study and are midway through another to examine more directly the role of attention in socioemotional selectivity. The first study was an attempt to investigate both individual and age differences in attention to emotional material simultaneously. At the same time that socioemotional selectivity theory researchers had found evidence for a positivity bias in the cognition of older individuals, optimism researchers were also investigating information processing. Research using an Emotional Stroop task found that optimistic young adults showed biased attention for positive stimuli (Segerstrom, 2001), whereas presenting potentially threatening information to optimistic individuals led researchers to conclude that the optimists engage with negative information even more than pessimists when it is relevant to them (Aspinwall & Brunhart, 1996). Using an eye tracker to measure visual attention could, therefore, provide some insight into how these individual and age differences in information processing interact in the service of emotion regulation.

The tracking system we use in the lab is an Applied Science Laboratories (ASL) Model 504 remote eye tracker with Magnetic Head Transmission to compensate for head position. Participants are seated approximately 20 in. in front of a 15-in. computer monitor, and the magnetic head transmitter is placed on a Velcro headband above the participant's left eye. Participants then complete a 9- or 17-point calibration procedure to ensure appropriate computer-based computations for their eye movements; then, they are ready to view stimuli and actually have their eyes tracked. Gaze position is recorded at 60 Hz, with an accuracy of better than 1° visual angle. *Fixations* are defined as gazes within 1° visual angle for at least 100 ms so that actual looking at parts of the screen can be distinguished from saccades, blinks, and other eye movements. Generally, we designate a part of the screen as an "area of interest" (AOI), and the eye tracker interface program will provide fixation data within that area for each participant.

Normal age-related changes in the eye make it especially challenging to use a bright pupil system such as the ASL eye tracker with older adult participants. To record successfully, the remote tracker needs an unobstructed view of the entire pupil. With age, pupils get smaller, eyelids droop, and lenses yellow; all of these factors make it difficult to track the eye movements of older participants (see Sekuler & Sekuler, 2000). But, it is not impossible: In this study, we successfully tracked 21 of our 31 older participants, for a 68% success rate. This is in comparison to our 89% success rate tracking young adult participants.

In the first set of studies I conducted using eye tracking to investigate attention to emotional images (Isaacowitz, in press), I selected skin cancer pictures as an unpleasant, negative image, because skin cancer had been used as a content area in some previous optimism research (e.g., Aspinwall & Brunhart, 1996) and because it is a health condition with a visual component. Participants in each of these studies were presented with a series of images of melanoma (skin cancer), as well as with schematic line drawings matched to each of the cancer images (to control for contours that draw attention) and female faces rated as neutral by external raters. Stimuli were presented in a standard order (face, lines, and cancer) so that participants would not form associations between skin cancers and their matched schematic line drawings. Stimuli were presented in the center of the screen for 15 s each, with 5 s of gray screen between presentations. Fixation to AOIs was recorded: the actual cancer in the melanoma images, the same areas in the matched schematic line drawings, and the face (hair to chin) in the neutral faces.

In addition to having their eye tracked as they viewed the presentation of images on the computer monitor, participants also completed a number of self-report demographic, personality, and affect measures. Included among these self-report questionnaires were the Life Orientation Test (LOT; Scheier & Carver, 1985) to measure dispositional optimism, the Center for Epidemiological Studies–Depression (CES–D) scale (Radloff, 1977) to assess current depressive mood, the Positive and Negative Scales (PANAS; Watson, Clark, & Tellegen, 1988) to measure current positive and negative affect, and a brief Neuroticism scale (Bolger & Schilling, 1991). Additionally, each participant reported on his or her family history of skin cancer as well as on the perceived relevance of skin cancer in his or her current life.

Originally we ran two samples of young adults (including a total of 53 men and 91 women) to investigate links between optimism and attention to negative information in that age group (Isaacowitz, in press). An overriding finding emerged:

More optimistic young adults showed less fixation time to the skin cancer images. This was true in more conservative tests in which attention to matched line drawings was controlled, as well as when the effects of affect were controlled. Young optimists, it seemed, selectively ignored unpleasant negative information.

Then, after modifying our setup to better accommodate aging eyes, we added our sample of older individuals. To examine age differences, we then compared these older individuals with those younger participants who had completed exactly the same protocol. All of these participants—young and old—had been instructed to view the images "naturally, as if at home watching television."

Several differences between the age groups emerged just on the self-report measures, which was consistent with previous findings (e.g., Mroczek & Kolarz, 1998; Regier et al., 1988). The older adults reported lower levels of depressive symptoms, higher levels of dispositional optimism, and more positive affect than did the young adults. However, no significant differences emerged for negative affect or neuroticism. Our older sample actually reported more years of education than did the younger sample, although there were no differences between the age groups in self-reported relevance of cancer.

Next, overall fixation data was analyzed for the different types of images. Interestingly, no age differences emerged on percentage of fixation to any of the three types of images. On a more conservative test using residual scores (after each skin cancer image had been regressed on its matched schematic line drawing), no age differences were found. Similarly, the age groups did not differ in their average number of saccades they made to the different stimuli.

Results became much more interesting when the role of the individual difference variable, optimism, was considered. A significant Age × Optimism effect emerged for skin cancer attention (controlling for attention to the matched drawings), $F(3, 92) = 3.05, p < .05$. Decomposing this interaction was somewhat challenging given the overall age difference in optimism. We ultimately pursued a strategy of investigating correlations between optimism and attention by age group to understand the interaction. In young adults, overall optimism scores were negatively correlated with residual scores indicating attentional preference toward the skin cancer images ($r = -.24, p < .05$), whereas in older adults the relationship was positive ($r = .49, p < .05$). A Fisher z test revealed that the difference between these two correlation coefficients was significant, $z = 2.81, p < .01$. Thus, whereas higher levels of optimism related to less attention toward the skin cancer in young adults, higher levels of optimism actually related to more attention to the unpleasant images in our older sample. An example of the effect in our older sample is presented in Figure 1, in which a more optimistic older individual gazes quite a bit at the cancer, whereas a less optimistic older adult gazes only slightly at it.

A lingering possible account for the age differences found in this study involves the effects of aging on vision, although admittedly it would be difficult to explain

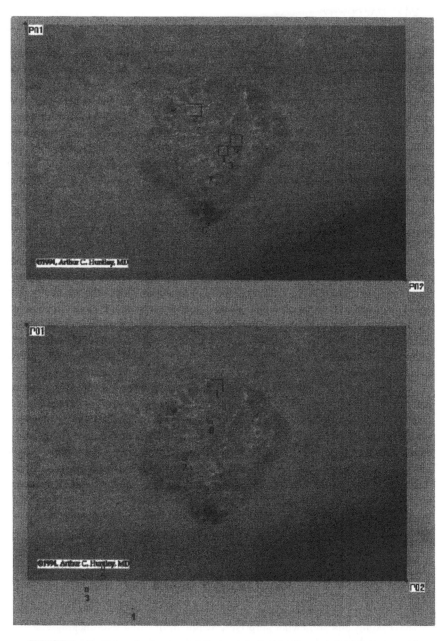

FIGURE 1 Examples of a more optimistic (top panel) and a less optimistic (bottom panel) older adult. Boxes indicate fixations within areas of interest; size of the box reflects time, so larger boxes indicate longer fixation times in that area. Numbers reflect fixation order (1 = first fixation, 2 = second fixation, etc.). Numbers outside the image reflect fixation to the gray screen surrounding the image. Reprinted with permission.

the particular Age × Optimism interaction using visual aging as the mechanism. Nonetheless, it seemed important both in terms of this particular study as well as to provide evidence for the utility of eye tracking as a tool for studying emotional development across the life span to be able to demonstrate that the effects were not merely due to age differences in vision. Two separate approaches to this issue were used in this study. The first was an individual difference approach: Each participant had completed two vision measures prior to having his or her eyes tracked. This approach involved testing visual acuity and contrast sensitivity in most of our older participants and a subset of our younger participants (young adults, $n = 27$; older adults, $n = 28$). The Snellen Test was used to assess visual acuity, and the Pelli–Robson Test measured contrast sensitivity in the left eye (Pelli, Robson, & Wilkins, 1988). Those participants in both age groups who did and did not have their vision tested did not differ on attention or optimism variables. Correlations between the vision measures and fixation were then calculated; contrast sensitivity did correlate with fixation patterns (such that better contrast sensitivity performance was related to more relative fixation to the skin cancer images), whereas acuity did not. The observed correlation with contrast sensitivity was in the same direction as the optimism effect in the older sample; thus, showing that optimism was not just an indirect proxy for a perceptual variable like contrast sensitivity seemed extremely important. However, covarying the effects of contrast sensitivity did not change the overall optimism–fixation results.

A psychophysical analysis of the skin cancer was the second approach used to determine whether age-related declines in contrast sensitivity might impact the results. Acuity was not investigated in depth because the images were large and centrally presented. Using a standard psychophysical judgment task ($n = 6$), the skin cancers were matched to increasing contrast gradients, and then the contrast judgments were fit to a second-order polynomial function. This yielded perceived contrast results for each of the five skin cancer images: Two images showed low contrast (under .50), whereas the other three showed high contrast. Considering these groups separately also did not impact the observed findings, suggesting that they were not simply the result of age differences in contrast sensitivity.

WHAT DOES IT MEAN?

After finding this somewhat surprising result in my first eye-tracking study of emotion and aging, I have tried to think critically about what the results might mean. These speculations have fallen into two primary categories—relevance and experience. The relevance account is the more straightforward of the two. Aspinwall (Aspinwall & Brunhart, 1996; Aspinwall, Richter, & Hoffman, 2001) has made a compelling case that optimists tune in more to negative information

·

when it is particularly relevant to them (e.g., vitamin users who view risk information about vitamins; Aspinwall & Brunhart, 1996). It may be the case that,
rather than there being any age effect per se in this study, the older individuals
simply find the topic of skin cancer to be more relevant to them, and optimists at-
tend more to bad news when it is relevant. The one piece of evidence from the
study that speaks against this explanation is that the age groups did not differ in
their self-ratings of how relevant skin cancer is to them.

Perhaps a more complicated, but also more compelling, account has to do with
the effects of age on experience processing emotional information. Human factors
research has shown that experience with certain attentional tasks can actually
change how attention works. So, for example, expert pilots and drivers look dif-
ferently at their environment than do novices (e.g., Crundell, Underwood, &
Chapman, 1999; L. J. Williams, 1995). One study found that postal workers who
sorted Canadian mail (in which the zip codes include both numbers and letters)
were faster at a search task involving distinguishing letters from numbers than
were their peers who sorted only American mail, with its number-only zip codes
(Polk & Farah, 1995). Clearly, experience and expertise can change attention.

One of the aforementioned assertions of socioemotional selectivity theory is
that older adults are experts at regulating their emotions. By working on emotions
and being oriented toward emotion regulation in goal pursuit, older individuals
may be emotion experts in a sense. This is also consistent with speculation as to
why older individuals have much lower rates of depression than their younger
counterparts (Regier et al., 1988). To explain this finding, Nolen-Hoeksema
(1988) suggested that older individuals may have developed better perspectives
when facing emotional problems; in other words, they have learned from experience that bad things are not quite so bad, and thus they become more in tune with
their emotions and better able to regulate them. Of course, this is also generally
consistent with the idea put forth in recent studies that older adults selectively
tune out information that might put them in a bad mood (e.g., Charles et al., 2003;
Mather & Carstensen, 2003). Moreover, there is always a selective survivorship
confound, as individuals who live longer certainly would have longer to learn and
benefit from experience.

All this speculation would be consistent with a main effect of age on fixation to
negative images, but how can it possibly explain the Age × Optimism interaction?
For this, one additional study bears consideration. This is Charles and colleagues'
(2001) study using data from the USC Generations Study. In this large study of
adults who were followed for up to 23 years, negative affect seemed to generally
decline with age, at least until age 60. Interestingly, however, one subgroup of individuals did not seem to display the age-related affective benefits found more
generally. This subgroup was those individuals high in the personality trait of
Neuroticism. Whereas the rest of the sample appeared better able to regulate their
moods to avoid negative affect as they got older, individuals high in Neuroticism

did not display any age-related improvement in their affective lives. One interpretation of these findings is that most individuals derived the experience-based improvement in perspective posited by Nolen-Hoeksema (1988), learning that things are often not as bad as they seem, and that they are resilient organisms who will recover from just about any stressor. The neurotic individuals may never learn that lesson: Their experiences may be the same, but just like anxious individuals can face the object of their anxiety many times without ever becoming less anxious about it (e.g., by believing things only turned out well because they closed their eyes, counted, or engaged in some other safety behavior; see Salkovskis, Clark, Hackmann, Wells, & Gelder, 1999), these neurotic individuals never learn that they are in fact quite affectively resilient.

The question of whether individuals can learn about how their affect system works from affective experiences has recently been taken up as part of the affective forecasting literature (e.g., T. D. Wilson, Meyers, & Gilbert, 2001). The gist of this work is that individuals are surprisingly inaccurate in predicting their affective responses to events; in particular, they appear to overestimate how long those responses will last (Gilbert, Pinel, Wilson, Blumberg, & Wheatley, 1998). Although none of the affective forecasting studies have directly investigated age effects, the effect has been found across several populations from young to middle adulthood (Gilbert et al., 1998). It appears, in data derived from lab-based experimental manipulations, that young adults do not learn from positive affective experiences, at least when *learning* is defined as becoming more accurate or less biased in predictions of future response (T. D. Wilson et al., 2001). In contrast, young adults do learn from negative affective experiences, although the authors argued that this is in part due to rationalization. Young adults in a negative feedback condition downgraded the quality and importance of the test on which they had received negative feedback, so their expectation that it would not bother them much in the future was considered to be a function of rationalizing their poor performance rather than actually learning about their response to it. Nonetheless, although the effects of experience on affect were modest in these studies, it does raise the possibility that, over time and over more significant affective experiences, individuals could become more accurate in their predictions about how they will respond to negative events.

How, then, can this help explain the optimism findings just described? Individuals high in Neuroticism tend to also be low in optimism (the correlation between the two across the two age groups in my study was substantial at −.47). Perhaps individuals high in optimism and low in Neuroticism—the ones who as young adults would have avoided looking at unpleasant, negative images such as those of skin cancer—have learned from experience that unpleasant information does not need to be avoided in order to not be troubling. Rather, they have learned that they can be resilient, particularly given opportunities for antecedent-oriented emotional regulation (Carstensen, Gross, & Fung, 1997; Gross et al., 1997), which would require early detection that something disturbing might come into view. Thus, the optimistic older individuals would be more likely to engage visually with an unpleasant image because they believe that engaging with possible problems is the best way to solve them.

Of course, expertise is not the only plausible mechanism by which experience could lead to the observed effects. Other possibilities include a simple habituation account, in which repeated exposure to a stimulus changes attention to it, or a mere exposure account. Although this all remains speculation, it does seem that simple habituation is the most parsimonious possible pathway, but the expertise account may be most plausible given the state of theory and research in the field.

CURRENT AND FUTURE STUDIES ON ATTENTION AND SOCIOEMOTIONAL AGING

The first goal for future studies is to further understand the age difference in attention to emotional stimuli. Although no overall age differences in attention to negative emotional stimuli were found in the first study we conducted, it is important to note that only negative and neutral stimuli were used. We are currently conducting a study to more directly investigate age differences in fixation to positive and negative emotional stimuli that may be more generally relevant (or irrelevant) than skin cancer images. In this study, participants view pairs of synthetic faces that have been designed either to show prototypic signs of a certain emotion (happiness, sadness, anger, or fear) or designed to be totally devoid of facial signs of emotion (Goren & Wilson, 2003; H. R. Wilson, Loffler, & Wilkinson, 2002). In each pair, the same individual face is presented: On one side the face is expressing an emotion, and on the other side the face is devoid of emotion. The left-to-right arrangement and order of emotions is counterbalanced. This study will provide a direct test of socioemotional selectivity theory's propositions about age differences, and it will help clarify the lack of main effects of age but the presence of an Age × Optimism interaction in our previous work.

We are currently planning and running several other studies to more directly disentangle the Age × Optimism interaction by testing the possible relevance and experience explanations for the effects observed. Rather than simply comparing the attentional patterns of adults of different ages, as in the studies described earlier, these studies instead try to get directly at the underlying mechanisms by modeling the age-related processes rather than observing them. So, for example, the relevance account will be investigated by selecting individuals of the same age who do and do not use artificial tanning and presenting them with information about skin cancer risk from artificial tanning as their eyes are tracked. If the relevance explanation is correct, optimistic individuals will look more at the skin cancer information if they are tanners but will look less at it if they are not.

These studies will involve investigating the origin of attentional preferences and biases and how these may help understand socioemotional functioning across the adult life span. In another set of studies, we plan to pursue the question of what these preferences and biases may mean in terms of actual health-related behavior. So, for example, if older individuals (particularly pessimistic ones) selectively ignore negative health-relevant information, are they actually less likely to practice health-promoting behavior? This work will help unravel how attention is and is not important in linking perception, cognition, emotion, and behavior in adulthood and old age.

ISSUES IN STUDYING AGE DIFFERENCES IN ATTENTION TO EMOTIONAL INFORMATION

Eye tracking is an exciting methodology for studying attention, but when differences between young and older adults are found in attentional patterns using eye tracking, an obvious concern is being able to demonstrate that the observed differences are actually about attention to emotion and not merely an artifact of age changes in vision or more general cognitive functioning. Thus, a battery of perceptual and cognitive measures are now included in each eye-tracking study. Vision measures include the tests of visual acuity and contrast sensitivity already described. More recently, a series of cognitive measures have also been added to each eye-tracking study of age differences. An important issue is delineating specific attentional preferences from general attentional functioning; therefore, a test of attentional performance, attentional inhibition, and attentional switching developed by Tun and Lachman (2003) known as the Red/Green task has been added to all studies. If observed attentional preferences with regard to emotional information remain significant when controlling for performance on the Red/Green task, then the presence of emotion-specific biases in attention can be more satisfactorily concluded. Additionally, Forward and Backward Digit Span and Digit Symbol Substitution tasks measure aspects of fluid intelligence and working memory, a Vocabulary task indexes crystallized intelligence, and the Mini-Mental State Exam allows for screening of early-stage dementia. Taken together, these tests will allow us to contextualize our attentional findings more generally within information processing across the adult life span.

CONCLUSIONS: IDENTIFYING TIME'S EYE

In search of the psychological processes underlying the ability of most older individuals to successfully regulate their emotions and to maintain high levels of well-being even as cognition and physical health may become more problematic, it seems clear that this affective success is no accident. It is instead the result of an orientation toward emotional goals that leads to antecedent-based emotion regulation (see Carstensen et al., 1997). However, it seems unlikely that these processes unfold in ways that involve completely thoughtful, volitional actions on the part of individuals; instead, it seems more plausible that at least part of the effects unfold more quickly and fundamentally as a part of information processing. The methodology described in this article represents an attempt to systematically investigate one part of information processing—namely, attention—that may be an area of interest when trying to understand age differences in emotion regulation. To the extent that eye tracking allows for measurement of attentional preferences and biases, this line of research may provide some sense of how cognition serves to promote socioemotional resilience as people age. The gift of time and personality may not be that they permit some people merely to think about and remember what they see in the world in a more positive manner, but rather time and personality may impact what stimuli from the world are seen at all.

ACKNOWLEDGMENTS

The research described in this article was supported by National Institute on Aging (NIA) Grant R03 AG22168–01.

I thank Laura Carstensen for valuable discussions on this topic, Heather Wadlinger for assistance with data collection and analysis, Robert Sekuler and Chris McLaughlin for help with the psychophysical analyses, and Art Huntley for his permission to use the skin cancer image.

REFERENCES

Aspinwall, L. G., & Brunhart, S. M. (1996). Distinguishing optimism from denial: Optimistic beliefs predict attention to health threats. *Personality and Social Psychology Bulletin, 22,* 993–1003.

Aspinwall, L. G., Richter, L., & Hoffman, R. R. (2001). Understanding how optimism "works": An examination of optimists' adaptive moderation of belief and behavior. In E. C. Chang (Ed.), *Optimism and pessimism: Theory, research, and practice* (pp. 217–238). Washington, DC: American Psychological Association.

Bolger, N., & Schilling, E. (1991). Personality and the problems of everyday life: The role of neuroticism in exposure and reactivity to daily stressors. *Journal of Personality, 59,* 355–386.

Carstensen, L. L. (1992). Social and emotional patterns in adulthood: Support for socioemotional selectivity theory. *Psychology and Aging, 7,* 331–338.

Carstensen, L. L. (1993). Motivation for social contact across the life span: A theory of socioemotional selectivity. In J. E. Jacobs (Ed.), *Nebraska Symposium on Motivation: Vol. 40. Developmental perspectives on motivation* (pp. 209–254). Lincoln: University of Nebraska Press.

Carstensen, L. L., & Fredrickson, B. L. (1998). The influence of HIV-status and age on cognitive representations of others. *Health Psychology, 17,* 494–503.

Carstensen, L. L., Gross, J., & Fung, H. (1997). The social context of emotion. In M. P. Lawton & K. W. Schaie (Eds.), *Annual review of geriatrics and gerontology* (pp. 325–352). New York: Springer.

Carstensen, L. L., Isaacowitz, D. M., & Charles, S. T. (1999). Taking time seriously: A theory of socioemotional selectivity. *American Psychologist, 54,* 155–181.

Carstensen, L. L., Pasupathi, M., Mayr, U., & Nesselroade, J. (2000). Emotion experience in everyday life across the adult life span. *Journal of Personality and Social Psychology, 79,* 644–655.

Carstensen, L. L., & Turk-Charles, S. (1994). The salience of emotion across the adult life course. *Psychology and Aging, 9,* 259–264.

Charles, S. T., Mather, M., & Carstensen, L. L. (2003). Aging and emotional memory: The forgettable nature of negative images for older adults. *Journal of Experimental Psychology: General, 132,* 310–324.

Charles, S. T., Reynolds, C. A., & Gatz, M. (2001). Age-related differences and change in positive and negative affect over 23 years. *Journal of Personality and Social Psychology, 80,* 136–151.

Cowan, N. (1988). Evolving conceptions of memory storage, selective attention and their mutual constraints within the human information-processing system. *Psychological Bulletin, 104,* 163–191.

Crundell, D., Underwood, G., & Chapman, P. (1999). Driving experience and the functional field of view. *Perception, 28,* 1075–1087.

Fung, H. H., & Carstensen, L. L. (2003). Sending memorable messages to the old: Age differences in preferences and memory for advertisements. *Journal of Personality and Social Psychology, 85,* 163–178.

Fung, H. H., Carstensen, L. L., & Lutz, M. A. (1999). Influence of time on social preferences: Implications for life-span development. *Psychology and Aging, 14,* 595–604.

Gilbert, D. T., Pinel, E. C., Wilson, T. D., Blumberg, S. J., & Wheatley, T. P. (1998). Immune neglect: A source of durability bias in affective forecasting. *Journal of Personality and Social Psychology, 75,* 617–638.

Goren, D., & Wilson, H. R. (2003). Quantifying recognition abilities for four major emotional expressions based on facial geometry [Abstract]. *Journal of Vision, 3*(9), 300a, http://journalofvision.org/3/9/300/, doi:10.1167/3.9.300.

Gould, O. N., & Dixon, R. A. (1993). How we spent our vacation: Collaborative storytelling by young and old adults. *Psychology and Aging, 8,* 10–17.

Gross, J., Carstensen, L. L., Pasupathi, M., Tsai, J., Götestam Skorpen, C., & Hsu, A. (1997). Emotion and aging: Experience, expression and control. *Psychology and Aging, 12,* 590–599.

Hashtroudi, S., Johnson, M. K., Vnek, N., & Ferguson, S. A. (1994). Aging and the effects of affective and factual focus on source monitoring and recall. *Psychology and Aging, 9,* 160–170.

Isaacowitz, D. M. (in press). The gaze of the optimist. *Personality and Social Psychology Bulletin.*

Isaacowitz, D. M., Charles, S. T., & Carstensen, L. L. (2000). Emotion and cognition. In F. I. M. Craik & T. A. Salthouse (Eds.), *The handbook of aging and cognition* (2nd ed., pp. 593–631). Mahwah, NJ: Lawrence Erlbaum Associates, Inc.

Isaacowitz, D. M., & Smith, J. (2003). Positive and negative affect in very old age. *Journal of Gerontology: Psychological Sciences, 58B,* P143–P152.

Kennedy, Q., Mather, M., & Carstensen, L. L. (2004). The role of motivation in the age-related positive bias in autobiographical memory. *Psychological Science, 15,* 208–214.

Lang, F. R., Staudinger, U. M., & Carstensen, L. L. (1998). Perspectives on socioemotional selectivity in late life: How personality and social context do (and do not) make a difference. *Journals of Gerontology: Psychological Science, 53B,* P21–P30.

Lawton, M. P., Kleban, M. H., Rajagopal, D., & Dean, J. (1992). Dimensions of affective experience in three age groups. *Psychology and Aging, 7,* 171–184.

Malatesta, C. Z., & Kalnok, M. (1984). Emotional experience in younger and older adults. *Journal of Gerontology, 39,* 301–308.

Masterpaqua, F., & Perna, P. A. (Eds.). (1997). *The psychological meaning of chaos.* Washington, DC: American Psychological Association.

Mather, M., & Carstensen, L. L. (2003). Aging and attentional biases for emotional faces. *Psychological Science, 14,* 409–415.

Mogg, K., & Marden, B. (1990). Selective processing of emotional information in anxious subjects. *British Journal of Clinical Psychology, 27,* 227–229.

Mogg, K., Millar, N., & Bradley, B. P. (2000). Biases in eye movements to threatening facial expressions in generalized anxiety disorder and depressive disorder. *Journal of Abnormal Psychology, 109,* 695–704.

Mroczek, D. K., & Kolarz, C. M. (1998). The effect of age on positive and negative affect: A developmental perspective on happiness. *Journal of Personality and Social Psychology, 75,* 1333–1349.

Nolen-Hoeksema, S. (1988). Life-span views on depression. In P. B. Baltes, D. L. Featherman, & R. L. Lerner (Eds.), *Life-span development and behavior* (Vol. 8, pp. 203–241). Hillsdale, NJ: Lawrence Erlbaum Associates, Inc.

Parkhurst, D., Law, K., & Niebur, E. (2002). Modeling the role of salience in the allocation of overt visual attention. *Vision Research, 42,* 107–123.

Pelli, D. G., Robson, J. G., & Wilkins, A. J. (1988). The design of a new letter chart for measuring contrast sensitivity. *Clinical Vision Science, 2,* 187–199.

Polk, T. A., & Farah, M. J. (1995). Late experience alters vision. *Nature, 376,* 648–649.

Radloff, L. S. (1977). The CES–D Scale: A self-report depression scale for use in the general population. *Applied Psychological Measurement, 1,* 385–401.

Regier, D. A., Boyd, J. H., Burke, J. D., Jr., Rae, D. S., Myers, J. K., Kramer, M., Robins, L. N., et al. (1988). One-month prevalence of mental disorders in the United States. *Archives of General Psychiatry, 45,* 977–986.

Revelle, W. (1993). Individual differences in personality and motivation: 'Non-cognitive' determinants of cognitive performance. In A. Baddeley & L. Weiskrantz (Eds.), *Attention: Selection, awareness, and control: A tribute to Donald Broadbent* (pp. 346–373). Oxford: Clarendon.

Salkovskis, P. M., Clark, D. M., Hackmann, A., Wells, A., & Gelder, M. G. (1999). An experimental investigation of the role of safety-seeking behaviours in the maintenance of panic disorder with agoraphobia. *Behaviour Research and Therapy, 37,* 559–574.

Scheier, M. F., & Carver, C. S. (1985). Optimism, coping, and health: Assessment and implications of generalized outcome expectancies. *Health Psychology, 4,* 219–247.

Schulz, R. (1985). Emotion and affect. In J. E. Birren & K. W. Schaie (Eds.), *Handbook of the psychology of aging* (2nd ed., pp. 531–543). New York: Van Nostrand Reinhold.

Segerstrom, S. C. (2001). Optimism and attentional bias for negative and positive information. *Personality and Social Psychology Bulletin, 2,* 1334–1343.

Sekuler, R., & Sekuler, A. B. (2000). Visual perception and cognition. In J. G. Evans, T. F. Williams, B. L. Beattle, J. -P. Michelm, & G. K. Wilcock (Eds.), *Oxford textbook of geriatric medicine* (2nd ed., pp. 874–880). Oxford, England: Oxford University Press.

Tun, P. A., & Lachman, M. E. (2003). *Test of Adult Cognition by Telephone (TACT)* (Tech. Rep.). Waltham, MA: Brandeis University.

Watson, D., Clark, L. A., & Tellegen, A. (1988). Development and validation of brief measures of positive and negative affect: The PANAS scales. *Journal of Personality and Social Psychology, 54,* 1063–1070.

Whitbourne, S. K. (2005). *Adult development and aging: Biopsychosocial perspectives* (2nd ed.). Hoboken, NJ: Wiley.

Williams, J. M. G., Watts, F. N., MacLeod, C., & Mathews, A. (1997). *Cognitive psychology and emotional disorders* (2nd ed.). New York: Wiley.

Williams, L. J. (1995). Peripheral target recognition and visual field narrowing in aviators and nonaviators. *The International Journal of Aviation Psychology, 5,* 215–232.

Wilson, H. R., Loffler, G., & Wilkinson, F. (2002). Synthetic faces, face cubes and the geometry of face space. *Vision Research, 42*, 2909–2923.

Wilson, T. D., Meyers, J., & Gilbert, D. T. (2001). Lessons from the past: Do people learn from experience that emotional reactions are short-lived? *Personality and Social Psychology Bulletin, 27*, 1648–1661.

Wood, N. L., Stadler, M. A., & Cowan, N. (1997). Is there implicit memory without attention? A reexamination of task demands in Eich's (1984) procedure. *Memory and Cognition, 25*, 772–779.

RESEARCH IN HUMAN DEVELOPMENT, 2(3), 133–158

What Can We Learn From Longitudinal Studies of Adult Development?

K. Warner Schaie
The Pennsylvania State University

This article distinguishes between normal and pathological aging, provides an interdisciplinary context, and then considers a sample case of cognitive aging. Developmental influences on cognition include the physiological infrastructure, genetic predispositions, and environmental influences. Different types of longitudinal studies are distinguished, and contrasting findings of cross-sectional and longitudinal studies are examined in the sample case of the Seattle Longitudinal Study. Also considered is the longitudinal context for intervention studies and the role of longitudinal family studies in assessing rate of aging and generational differences in rates of aging. Finally, attention is given to the role of longitudinal studies in the early detection of risk for dementia in advanced age.

In this article I distinguish between normal and pathological aging, provide some historical context, discuss shifts in relevant methodological paradigms, provide an interdisciplinary context, and then consider a sample case of cognitive aging in greater detail.

A distinction is made between age-related declines that should be attributed either to neuropathology or to disuse and obsolescence. But aging can also be considered as development in domains such as experience and wisdom, and we must distinguish between successful and unsuccessful aging.

The study of adult development originated in the early mental testing movement. Cross-sectional findings of substantial age-related declines from early to late adulthood soon motivated the development of longitudinal studies. Other methodological paradigm shifts of importance to longitudinal inquiry have involved advances in the measurement of age, confirmatory factor analysis, and treatment of age as the dependent variable.

Requests for reprints should be sent to K. Warner Schaie, Evan Pugh Professor of Human Development and Psychology, The Pennsylvania State University, 135 Nittany Ave., Suite 405, State College, PA 16801. E-mail: kws@psu.edu

I then present a model that considers the roles of age-related changes in the physiological infrastructure, genetic predispositions, and environmental influences. Different types of longitudinal studies are distinguished, and contrasting findings of cross-sectional and longitudinal studies are examined in the sample case of the Seattle Longitudinal Study.

Selected findings from this study are presented to discuss the complex interaction of longitudinal age changes and cohort differences. The latter introduces the role of longitudinal family studies in assessing rate of aging and generational differences in rates of aging. Also, I briefly consider the longitudinal context for intervention studies designed to slow the rate of aging.

And, finally, I discuss the role of longitudinal studies in the early detection of risk for dementia in advanced age, which involves linkages between studies of normal and pathological aging as well as attention to genetic markers of dementia.

NORMAL AND PATHOLOGICAL AGING

There is considerable controversy in the developmental sciences regarding whether it is possible to conceptualize aging free of age-related diseases (cf. Solomon, 1999). There are vast individual differences in the age of onset, the particular disease(s) an individual experiences, and the severity of chronic disease in old age. Nevertheless, one of the concomitants of reaching advanced ages is the presence of more or less disabling chronic disease. It may be more useful, therefore, to distinguish between those aspect of aging that involve decline and/or functional losses and those processes that can be characterized as developmental gains occurring with advancing age.

Aging as Decline

One of the most popular models guiding discussions of human aging and behavior involves the assumption that there is an accelerating linear decline for most behaviors past an asymptote occurring somewhere in adolescence or young adulthood. This model is informed primarily by cross-sectional data. It does not account for the fact that different behaviors have been found to have divergent developmental courses through adulthood or that longitudinal data often have nonlinear growth curves in adulthood.

The substantial age differences observed at a given point in time that often, but not always, favor young adults over the elderly can perhaps be best accounted for by three co-occurring phenomena: neuropathology, disuse, and obsolescence.

Neuropathology.   It has been observed that there are age changes in volume of various brain structures occurring in normal individuals with advancing age (Gunning-Dixon & Raz, 2003; Raz, Rodrigue, & Acker, 2003). Excess volumetric decline in brain tissues may indeed be a precursor of clinically diagnosable neuropathology. These brain changes are associated as well with decline in cognitive functioning. Recent work in our laboratory has shown that excess cognitive change can be identified as early as 14 years prior to neuropsychological diagnosis of cognitive impairment (Schaie et al., 2005). Hence, with increasing age, there will also be an increase in the proportion of individuals whose behavior is impaired due to the precursors of neuropathology.

Disuse.   Following the principles of selective optimization and compensation (cf. Baltes, 1997; Baltes & Baltes, 1990), we would expect that aging individuals would progressively increase their efforts on maintaining those behaviors that are most adaptive and meaningful for their particular life situation. Because some skills and behaviors are neglected in this process, we would expect increasing proportions of elderly to show decline that may well be reversible (cf. Willis, 2001).

Obsolescence.   In a rapidly changing society, skills that are acquired at earlier points in life may quickly become obsolete, particularly in the presence of rapid technological change (Charness & Schaie, 2003; Pew & Van Hemel, 2004; Willis & Dubin, 1990). The resultant obsolescence, in turn, leads to the avoidance of behaviors and social or work roles that now depend on more effective behaviors or higher skill levels than those attained asymptotically in young adulthood. Enhancing this obsolescence is a tendency of employers to give preference to younger employees for on-the-job training or other updating experiences (cf. Czaja, 2001; Schaie & Schooler, 1998). Hence, in the age-comparative literature older groups will have successively larger proportions of members who have not declined but appear obsolete when compared with their younger peers.

Aging as Development

Not all comparisons of the young and the old result in findings that are unfavorable for the elderly. There are a number of time-dependent processes that accompany living for a long time that result in favorable outcomes. Of particular interest here is the fact that it requires time to acquire the experience necessary for complex processes and societal roles, something that is often discussed and researched under the topic of *wisdom* (Staudinger, Maciel, Smith, & Baltes, 1998; Sternberg & Lubart, 2001). But there are other behavioral developments that include the adoption or neglect of favorable lifestyles as well as the development of flexible response styles and appropriate management of stress and emotional conflicts. All of the latter developments have been studied with the intention of differentiating successful from unsuccessful aging (cf. Rowe & Kahn, 1987). Identification of the major influences involved in this differentiation, often first discernible in midlife, requires long-term longitudinal data (cf. Arbuckle, Maag, Pushkar, & Chaikelson, 1998; Schaie, 1984; Schaie & Hofer, 2001; Willis & Reid, 1999).

SOME HISTORICAL CONTEXT

Longitudinal studies of behavioral change over the life span did not occur in a vacuum. They originated from the early mental testing movement and the age-comparative studies that presented difficulties in interpreting the course of individual development.

The Mental Testing Movement: Binet and Terman

Early research in developmental psychology began with the investigation of intellectual competence. Objectives of this line of research included devising orderly procedures for the removal of mentally retarded children from the public schools (Binet & Simon, 1905) and studying the distribution of individual differences in the interest of demonstrating their Darwinian characteristics (Galton, 1869). The methods to describe developmental status of individuals were brought to the United States by Lewis Terman with his introduction of the widely used Stanford–Binet Intelligence Test (1916) and the concepts of mental age and the IQ.

Empirical studies of intelligence that followed investigated how complex mental functions were acquired early in life (Brooks & Weintraub, 1976). Soon interest arose in following intellectual development beyond childhood, beginning with the theoretical expositions of G. Stanley Hall (1922), H. L. Hollingsworth (1927), and Sidney Pressey (Pressey, Janney, & Kuhlen, 1939). These authors raised questions concerned with identifying the age of attaining peak performance levels, maintenance or transformation of intellectual structures, and decremental changes thought to occur from young adulthood to old age.

Early Age-Comparative Studies of Adults

Developmental studies began with comparing the characteristics of groups of individuals of different ages at one point in time (cross-sectional studies). In his original standardization of the Binet tests for American use, Terman (1916) assumed that intellectual development reached a peak at age 16 and would then remain level throughout adulthood. However, large-scale studies of American soldiers using the Army Alpha Intelligence Test during World War I (Yerkes, 1921) suggested that the peak level of intellectual functioning for young adults, on average, might already be reached by age 13.

Other empirical studies questioned these inferences. One of the most influential cross-sectional studies, by Jones and Conrad (1933), collected data on most inhabitants of a New England community between the ages of 10 and 60 years. Age differences found in this study were quite substantial on some of the subtests of the Army Alpha Intelligence Test but not on others. In a similar fashion, Wechsler's (1939) initial standardization studies for the Wechsler–Bellevue Adult Intelligence scales found that growth of intelligence does not cease in adolescence. In fact, peak ages were found to differ for various aspects of intellectual functioning, and decrements at older ages were clearly not uniform across different subtests. The progressive shift in peak age of performance was perhaps the first harbinger of the now familiar problem of cohort differences that compromise the utility of cross-sectional inquiry to provide a model of developmental phenomena.

SHIFT IN METHODOLOGICAL PARADIGMS

Next, I consider the shifts in methodological paradigms that have characterized the study of human development. Those covered here are the shift from cross-sectional to longitudinal study designs, advances in the measurement of change, the shift from exploratory to confirmatory (hypothesis-testing) methods of factor analysis, and the reconceptualization of calendar age from its status as an independent (causal) variable to that of a dependent variable or temporal scale along which an outcome occurs.

Cross-Sectional to Longitudinal Design

In the late 1920s some developmental psychologists began to realize that age-comparative studies did not permit studying the association of antecedent and consequent variables over time in order to discover the mechanisms that accounted for individual development. Panels of children and their parents were, therefore, selected with the intent of systematic follow-up across time (e.g., Berkeley Growth Study; Eichorn, Clausen, Haan, Honzik, & Mussen, 1981).

By the 1950s reports appeared on longitudinal studies of individuals who had initially been studied as children or young adults and who had now reached middle adulthood (e.g., Bayley & Oden, 1955; Jarvik, Kallman, & Falek, 1962; Owens, 1953, 1959). Findings from these studies provided strong evidence that most abilities were maintained at least into midlife and that some abilities remained stable into early old age. These findings clearly contrasted with the results of the earlier cross-sectional literature, including my own findings (Schaie, 1958, 1959).

Further analyses of the conflicting evidence from cross-sectional and longitudinal data suggested that cross-sectional data representing age differences can model change over time only in the case of a perfectly stable environment and the absence of cohort differences (Ryder, 1965; Schaie, 1965). Although both cross-sectional and longitudinal approaches face a variety of different validity threats (cf. Schaie, 1977, 2005), it is clear that longitudinal data are preferred under most circumstances (cf. Baltes & Nesselroade, 1979).

The principal advantage of longitudinal studies is their ability to furnish information on intraindividual change in contrast to cross-sectional studies that provide information only on interindividual differences. Five distinct rationales for longitudinal studies have been suggested by Baltes and Nesselroade (1979; also see Schaie, 1983). They include the direct identification of intraindividual change, the identification of interindividual variability in intraindividual change, the interrelationships among intraindividual changes, the analysis of determinants of intraindividual change, and the analysis of intraindividual variability in the determinants of intraindividual change.

Advances in the Measurement of Change

The second paradigm shift with major impact on the study of adult development occurred in the field of measurement of change, which is so essential for defining developmental transitions. It began with some heated debates of the problem that measurement imperfections (i.e., deviations of observed scores from true scores) were likely to cumulate in gain (or loss) scores comparing multiple measurements of the same individuals (Lord, 1956; Thorndike, 1924). During the 1960s many developmentalists despaired about whether it was even possible to assess change adequately (cf. Cronbach & Furby, 1970; Harris, 1963). However, difference scores have always been important in studies of adult development that require tests of hypotheses about directional change. Fortunately, the problem of the unreliability of difference scores is usually confined to two-point studies, thus leading to increasing preference for multiple-occasion studies (cf. Nesselroade, Stigler, & Baltes, 1980; Rogosa, Brandt, & Zimowsky, 1982; Willett, 1989).

When longitudinal studies are conducted over long periods of time with multiple measurements, it is possible to apply powerful methods of linear growth curve modeling that allow separating patterns of individual change over time from the group averages that had previously represented the primary focus of inquiry. These methods also allow incorporating covariates and predictors of different forms of development. Multivariate growth curve methods were first introduced by Tucker (1958). But more powerful computational resources were required to implement currently popular approaches of multilevel modeling (cf. Bryk & Raudenbush, 1987; Rogosa & Willett, 1985; Rudinger & Rietz, 2001; Willett & Sayer, 1994). These methods are particularly useful because differences in genetic predisposition and environmental exposure may result in longitudinal aging patterns that differ markedly for subsets of the population, including groups of individuals with either favorable or unfavorable life experiences.

Exploratory to Confirmatory Factor Analysis

The method of exploratory factor analysis was developed as a way of organizing domains of variables such that a minimum number of latent constructs could explain and represent a large universe of observable behaviors in a psychologically meaningful fashion (e.g., Thurstone, 1947). A perennial problem of exploratory factor analysis has been the fact that there are an infinite number of alternate sets of equations that can account equally well for the regression of the latent factors on a particular set of observed variables.

The introduction of formal methods of confirmatory factor analysis and structural equation modeling facilitated the use of this method for testing hypotheses regarding developmental change. Thus, it is now possible to examine formally the proposition that there are differences in psychological constructs across samples of different age or within the same sample over time (cf. Reinert, 1970; Sörbom & Jöreskog, 1978).

It is now possible to assess systematically the invariance (stability) of the regression of the latent constructs on the observed variables. In studies of adult development such invariance is a singular prerequisite for the comparison of individuals and groups over long periods of time or the comparison of groups of different individuals who differ in salient characteristics. Confirmatory factor analysis can also be used to test hypotheses about the differentiation and dedifferentiation of psychological domains across the adult life span (Baltes & Lindenberger, 1997; Maitland, Intrieri, Schaie, & Willis, 2000; Reinert, 1970; Schaie, 2000; Schaie, Maitland, Willis, & Intrieri, 1998).

Age: From Independent to Dependent Variable

Another paradigmatic shift has occurred suggesting that developmentalists should treat chronological (calendar) age as a dependent rather than as an independent variable. First introduced conceptually by Wohlwill (1973), behavioral scientists soon began to realize that the study of age or duration time as a dependent variable could be operationalized via methods of survival or event-time analysis (Allison, 1984; Schaie, 1989; Singer & Willett, 1991). This approach has also been important in cognitive and health psychology, because the prediction of morbidity and mortality by means of earlier behavioral characteristics requires not only the definition of end points but also the timing (i.e., age) at which such end points are most likely to occur (e.g., Bosworth, Schaie, Willis, & Siegler, 1999). We have begun to recognize that the passage of time and getting older cannot have any causal property for any observed behavior change. Instead, we seek to identify and understand those causal variables and covariates that provide the mechanisms for change. Given these considerations, chronological age then becomes a scale on which we can arrange the timing of developmental events conditional to the specific characteristics of the individual under observation.

TYPES OF LONGITUDINAL STUDIES

Three different formats may be found in the literature. The first involves the adult follow-up of samples collected for studies of child development, the second explicitly covers the entire period of adulthood, and the third involves studies that begin by obtaining samples of the old or very old (cf. Schaie & Hofer, 2001).

From Early Childhood to Adulthood

The earliest longitudinal studies depict panels whose members had been recruited at birth or in early childhood and who were successively followed into young adulthood and midlife (e.g., the Berkeley Growth and Guidance Studies; Eichorn et al., 1981). These studies have been historically important, and they also can inform regarding those early influences that may differentially affect behavioral outcomes at later life stages. However, because no such studies were designed to continue into middle or old age, they often lack information on critical variables, such as the early precursors of cardiovascular disease that may be unimportant in childhood but may have important predictive value for later life.

From Young Adulthood to Midlife and Beyond

Other studies explicitly wish to cover the entire range of adulthood. They often begin as a cross-sectional study covering a wide age range and then continue as multiple birth cohorts (cf. Schaie, 1996, 2005). Such studies focus on variables and processes occurring in young adulthood and midlife that are suspected of contributing to the divergent developmental paths seen in old age. As new relationships among developmental processes are discovered and as new assessment tools become available, long-range data from such studies also allow postdicting developmental processes for variables that could not be assessed at earlier measurement occasions. Hence, these studies as they persist over long periods of time may give us an understanding of gains occurring from young adulthood into middle age as well as provide early predictions of risk of late-life decline and pathologies.

Studies Originating in Later Life

The largest number of longitudinal studies of adults have actually originated when participants were at advanced ages. These studies were initiated to understand the vast individual differences in aging patterns and in neuropathology in the elderly. Such studies have typically recruited their samples in the late 60s or early 70s, but there are also studies that have provided initial looks at octogenarians and even centenarians. Noteworthy examples of such studies are the Duke Longitudinal Study (Palmore, Busse, Maddox, Nowlin, & Siegler, 1985), the Swedish Betula Study (Nilsson et al., 1997), the German Berlin Aging Study (BASE; Baltes & Mayer, 1999), and the Victoria Longitudinal Study (Hultsch, Hertzog, Dixon, & Small, 1998).

THE SAMPLE CASE OF COGNITIVE DEVELOPMENT: A CONCEPTUAL MODEL

I now illustrate some of the advantages of longitudinal studies of development by examining some design features and data from the Seattle Longitudinal Study (SLS; Schaie, 1996, 2005). To begin, I describe a conceptual model of adult cognitive development that is currently guiding this study and that also provides an illustration of the interdisciplinary context that informs longitudinal studies of behavioral development (see Figure 1).

Cognitive development from early adulthood to old age cannot be understood adequately without examining such development within the context of changing environmental influences and changes in individuals' physiological infrastructure. The schematic displayed in Figure 1 indicates how these influences might operate over the adult life course. The schematic contains two end points: The first concerns the level of late-life cognitive functioning, and a second end point represents the status of the cortex at life's end. The latter end point describes the physiological infrastructure required for the maintenance of cognitive functioning, most reliably determinable only at post mortem. Although future work might include imaging techniques at earlier life stages, the conceptual model uses the typical conventions of path models. Rectangles identify those individual indicators that are observed directly, whereas ovals indicate the latent constructs inferred from sets of observed variables (not specified in this heuristic model).

The initial bases for the development of adult intelligence must be attributed to both heritable (genetic) influences and early environmental influences experienced within the home of the biological parents. The older behavior genetic literature suggests that much of the early environmental variance is not shared (e.g., Plomin & Daniels, 1987), but there is recent retrospective evidence that some early shared environmental variance influences later cognitive performance (Schaie & Zuo, 2001). Both genetic and early environmental factors are thought to influence midlife cognitive functioning. Both shared and not-shared environmental influences in early life exert influences on midlife social status (Nguyen, 2000). But environmental influences do not cease in adulthood. Indeed, attributes of the current family environment account for a substantial share of variance in

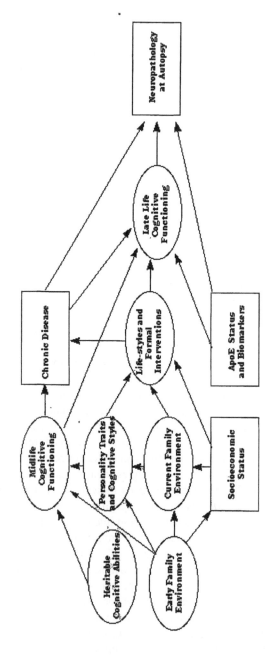

FIGURE 1   Conceptual model of factors associated with adult cognitive development. From *Developmental Influences on Adult Intelligence: The Seattle Longitudinal Study* (p. 8), by K. W. Schaie, 2005, New York: Oxford University Press. Copyright 2005 Oxford University Press. Adapted with permission.

midlife cognitive performance (Schaie & Zuo, 2001). Genetic factors are also likely to be implicated in the rate of cognitive decline in adulthood. Thus far the best-studied gene in this context is the Apo-E gene, one of whose alleles (e4) is a risk factor for Alzheimer's disease. Apo-E status is, therefore, added as a factor; the expression of the gene is probably not at issue prior to midlife.

The causal influences that determine the level of intellectual functioning in late life as well as cortical status at autopsy are also specified in the model. The direct influences implicated, in addition to genes whose expression is turned on in late life, most likely originate in midlife. They include level of midlife cognitive functioning, midlife life styles, and the incidence and severity of chronic disease. But there are indirect influences attributable to the effects of midlife cognitive function and lifestyles on chronic disease, as well as shared family influences on midlife cognition and of social status on midlife life styles.

Some of the paths shown in Figure 1 represent concurrent observations that would allow alternative reciprocal causal directions. However, most of the paths specified by the model represent antecedent–consequent relationships that require longitudinal data for their estimation and understanding. Over the course of the SLS most of the influences specified in this model either have already been systematically investigated or are currently under investigation.

THE SLS

The SLS began in 1956 with a cross-sectional inquiry of the relation between flexibility–rigidity and cognitive abilities over the age range from 20 to 70 years (Schaie, 1958). It was converted to a multiple-cohort longitudinal study in 1963, and it has been continued in 7-year intervals, adding new random samples from the membership of a large health maintenance organization (HMO). In the longitudinal part of the study members are followed until death or dropout, and our oldest study participant is now 100 years old. Figure 2 shows the sampling plan for data collected from 1956 through 1998.

Study Objectives

Although the initial objective of the SLS was to contribute to the problem of differentiating age changes and age differences, efforts soon turned to the identification of antecedents of individual differences in aging. Influences studied in the SLS include the following: occurrence of chronic disease, lifestyles and leisure activities, cognitive styles, personality traits, environment in family of origin and current family, and health behaviors. Given the multicohort nature of our sample we then studied generational differences in performance level and rate of decline at comparable ages. With the collaboration of behavior geneticists we then began

Study Waves

1956	1963	1970	1977	1984	1991	1998
S_1T_1 (N = 500)	S_1T_2 (N = 302)	S_1T_3 (N = 163)	S_1T_4 (N = 130)	S_1T_5 (N = 97)	S_1T_6 (N = 75)	S_1T_7 (N = 38)
	S_2T_2 (N = 997)	S_2T_3 (N = 419)	S_2T_4 (N = 333)	S_2T_5 (N = 225)	S_2T_6 (N = 163)	S_2T_7 (N = 111)
		S_3T_3 (N = 705)	S_3T_4 (N = 337)	S_3T_5 (N = 224)	S_3T_6 (N = 175)	S_3T_7 (N = 127)
			S_4T_4 (N = 609)	S_4T_5 (N = 293)	S_4T_6 (N = 203)	S_4T_7 (N = 136)
				S_5T_5 (N = 629)	S_5T_6 (N = 427)	S_5T_7 (N = 266)
					S_6T_6 (N = 693)	S_6T_7 (N = 406)
						S_7T_7 (N = 719)

S = Sample; T = Time of Measurement

FIGURE 2   Design of the SLS.

to pursue the role of family similarity in cognition, including the impact of family environment on cognition (e.g., Schaie et al., 1993; Schaie & Zuo, 2001). The family study is now in its third wave, generating longitudinal data that can be compared to our original longitudinal panel.

Having identified some of the antecedents of favorable and unfavorable change in adult cognition, we began to design cognitive intervention studies to slow or reverse cognitive decline in old age (Willis & Schaie, 1986), with studies of long-range effects up to 14 years (Schaie, 2005). And, finally, we have investigated precursors of cognitive impairment with neuropsychological studies and identification of ApoE gene status. These studies are beginning to contribute to the early identification of persons at risk for dementia.

Abilities Studied

The following six multiply marked cognitive ability factors were studied:

1. *Verbal Ability* is the ability to understand ideas expressed in words. It indicates the range of a person's passive vocabulary used in activities wherein information is obtained by reading or listening.
2. *Spatial Orientation* is the ability to visualize and mentally manipulate spatial configurations in two or three dimensions, to maintain orientation with respect to spatial objects, and to perceive relationships among objects in space. This ability is important in tasks that require deducing one's physical orientation from a map or visualizing what objects would look like when assembled from pieces.

· 3. *Inductive Reasoning* is the ability to recognize and understand novel concepts or relationships; it involves the solution of logical problems—to foresee and plan. Thurstone and Thurstone (1949) proposed that persons with good reasoning ability could solve problems, foresee consequences, analyze situations on the basis of past experience, and make and carry out plans according to recognized facts.
4. *Numeric Facility* is the ability to understand numerical relationships, to work with figures, and to solve simple quantitative problems rapidly and accurately.
5. *Perceptual Speed* is the ability to find figures, make comparisons, and carry out other simple tasks involving visual perception with speed and accuracy.
6. *Verbal Memory* is the ability that involves memorization and recall of meaningful language units primarily measured by memorizing lists.

LONGITUDINAL AGE CHANGES

We now contrast the longitudinal age changes obtained by studying intraindividual change over time with age differences measured for different age groups at one point in time for the six abilities averaged across the same cohorts used for the intraindividual change estimates.

Note first that in the cross-sectional data, reflecting interindividual age differences, four of the six factors show consistent negative age differences (see Figure 3). They are statistically significant for Inductive Reasoning, Spatial Orientation, and Perceptual Speed at age 46 and for Verbal Memory at age 39. The magnitude of age difference from the youngest to the oldest group amounts to approximately 2 *SD*s on average. The remaining two factors, Numeric Facility and Verbal Ability, have a very different profile. They both show positive age differences until midlife, with less than 0.5 *SD* negative differences thereafter, such that persons in advanced old age, on average, are at a higher level than the youngest age group.

Now we examine the age changes as obtained from intraindividual data (shown in Figure 4). These gradients are centered on the actually observed mean for the average age group in our sample (age 53). A rather different picture emerges for the longitudinal data. For these ability factor scores, earliest reliably observed decline over 7 years occurs for Perceptual Speed and Numeric Facility by age 60; for Inductive Reasoning, Spatial Orientation, and Verbal Memory by age 67; and for Verbal Ability only by age 81.

Contrasting the Cross-Sectional and Longitudinal Findings

The cross-sectional data obviously misinform if they were to be taken as estimates of decline in cognitive abilities. In the longitudinal data both the peak of performance and the age at which significant average decline is first noted occurs much

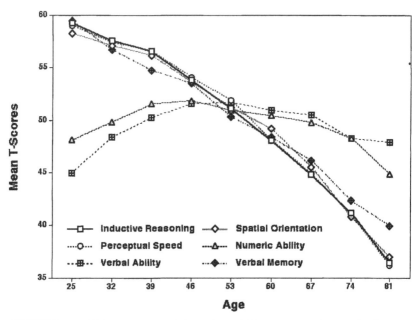

FIGURE 3   Age difference patterns of six cognitive abilities. From *Developmental Influences on Adult Intelligence: The Seattle Longitudinal Study* (p. 103), by K. W. Schaie, 2005, New York: Oxford University Press. Copyright 2005 Oxford University Press. Reprinted with permission.

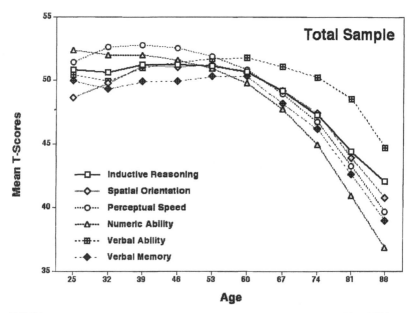

FIGURE 4   Estimated age changes from 7-year intraindividual data for six cognitive abilities. From *Developmental Influences on Adult Intelligence: The Seattle Longitudinal Study* (p. 127), by K. W. Schaie, 2005, New York: Oxford University Press. Copyright 2005 Oxford University Press. Reprinted with permission.

146

later. But there are also other surprises. Perhaps the most dramatic difference between the cross-sectional and longitudinal findings is for Numeric Facility. Here we see only minor differences among age groups in the cross-sectional data in contrast to the longitudinal data that show that there is early and steep decline for this ability.

How can we explain these differences? The major culprits here are cohort or generational differences. That is, if there is a positive cohort difference, then in cross-sectional studies older people will look as if they had declined from an earlier peak performance even though they have remained stable. By contrast, if there are negative cohort differences, older persons will appear to have remained stable in cross-sectional studies even though they have experienced marked decline from their peak. To address this issue we turn next to the study of generational differences.

STUDYING GENERATIONAL DIFFERENCES

Multicohort studies are required to determine whether there are differences in performance level obtained by successive cohorts at identical ages. Alternatively, we can compare biologically related individuals if we have access to data collected at similar ages for parents and offspring.

Cohort Studies

Cross-national studies of successive cohorts of school children have found substantial increments in intellectual performance over the past century (Flynn, 1987). Similar findings have occurred in the SLS. However, our ability-specific data suggest that cohort differences may occur in a multidirectional manner. Our latest findings for the six cognitive abilities described earlier are presented in Figure 5.

Over the 70-year range covered by our cohort data, substantial positive and linear cohort differences were observed for the Inductive Reasoning and Perceptual Speed abilities (~1 SD). A similar, albeit less steep, positive difference pattern occurred for Spatial Orientation (0.6 SD) and Verbal Memory (0.7 SD). A modest negative gradient (0.5 SD) was found for Numeric Facility, and there was a modest concave gradient with recent declines for Verbal Ability. These are exactly the abilities that appear flat in cross-sectional studies (as previously mentioned).

Family Studies

We also examined generational differences in cognitive abilities using the parent–offspring data from our family study (Schaie, Plomin, Willis, Gruber-Baldini, & Dutta, 1992). To permit matching parents and offspring at similar ages we re-

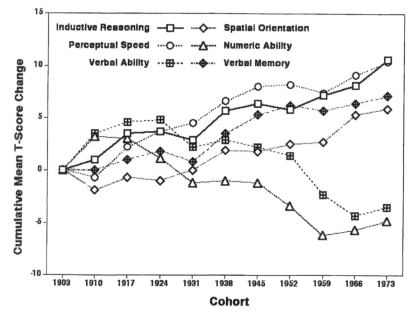

FIGURE 5   Cohort difference gradients for the six cognitive abilities. From *Developmental Influences on Adult Intelligence: The Seattle Longitudinal Study* (p. 144), by K. W. Schaie, 2005, New York: Oxford University Press. Copyright 2005 Oxford University Press. Reprinted with permission.

ported data on five single-marker ability tests: Verbal Meaning, Space, Reasoning, Number, and Word Fluency (Schaie, 1985). Figure 6 shows differences between the parent and offspring generations; a bar above the zero line indicates the advantage of the offspring over their parents, and a bar below the zero line indicates an advantage for the parents.

Consistent with the general population data, the offspring generation performed significantly better than their parents at comparable ages on Verbal Meaning, Space, and Reasoning, whereas the parent generation did better than their offspring on Number and Word Fluency.

Rate of Cognitive Change

Longitudinal studies also allow the investigation of cohort and generational differences in rate of cognitive change. A policy-relevant aspect of our generational studies is the possibility of asking whether the rate of aging has changed across successive generations. Recent policy debates in the United States and Europe have asked the question whether Social Security and other pension systems will remain viable when the Baby Boomers reach retirement. A straightforward solution for this problem would be to raise the age at which pensions are now paid (cf. Crystal & Shea, 2002). However, such an approach requires the assumption that

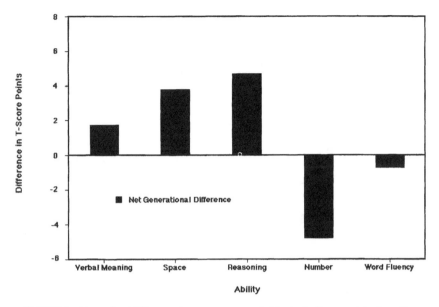

FIGURE 6   Generational differences between parents and offspring in *T*-score points. From *Developmental Influences on Adult Intelligence: The Seattle Longitudinal Study* (p. 335), by K. W. Schaie, 2005, New York: Oxford University Press. Copyright 2005 Oxford University Press. Adapted with permission.

the next generation is able to work to later ages because the rate of aging has slowed. That is, will the next generation decline physically and mentally more slowly than their parents?

The most direct test of whether the rate of cognitive aging has slowed is provided by the comparison of persons with their biologically related adult offspring at approximately the same ages. We now have a relevant data set in the SLS. To obtain approximate age equivalence, we compared the 1970 and 1977 test scores of the parents with the 1990 and 1997 test scores of the adult offspring. Figure 7 shows the 7-year change from the mid-60s to the early 70s. As previously shown, the offspring generation has typically higher levels of performance than their parents. More noteworthy, however, is the fact that although the parent generation declined significantly over the 7-year period on five of six abilities, the offspring generation showed decline on only two of six abilities.

COGNITIVE INTERVENTIONS TO SLOW AGING

Longitudinal studies lend themselves to the design and implementation of cognitive interventions because they can identify mechanisms involved in age-related change. They also allow the determination of whether any obtained training gain

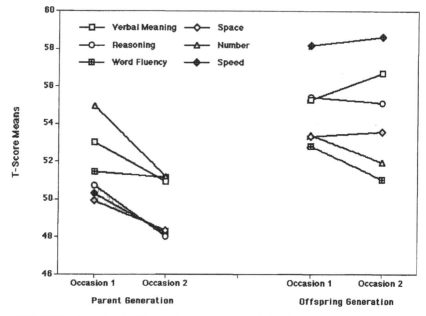

FIGURE 7   Generational differences between parents and offspring by cohort. From *Developmental Influences on Adult Intelligence: The Seattle Longitudinal Study* (p. 336), by K. W. Schaie, 2005, New York: Oxford University Press. Copyright 2005 Oxford University Press. Reprinted with permission.

is a function of remediating decline from a previous higher level of functioning or whether they simply "teach old dogs new tricks." The latter, of course, is not to be eschewed lightly because training gains in cognitive skills may well be important in facilitating obsolescence-reducing activities by the elderly. Important issues in intervention research are the determination of the specific targets of the intervention, the question of whether there is transfer of training to the broader dimensions being targeted, and whether there is maintenance of the effects of the intervention over time (see Willis, 2001).

Results of Cognitive Training

In the SLS, we conducted a cognitive training study as part of our 1984, 1991, and 1998 cycles. Participants age 64 and older were screened on whether they had remained stable or had experienced significant decline on the Inductive Reasoning and Spatial Orientation factors over the previous 14 years. Individuals who had declined only on one ability were assigned to training on that ability, whereas those who had remained stable or who had declined on both abilities received random assignment to the two training conditions. One-on-one strategy training was conducted in five 1-hr sessions. Figure 8 shows training gains for the three replications.

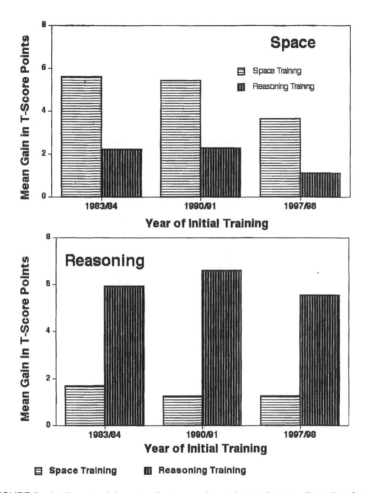

FIGURE 8   Replicated training gains for intervention and control groups. From *Developmental Influences on Adult Intelligence: The Seattle Longitudinal Study* (p. 175), by K. W. Schaie, 2005, New York: Oxford University Press. Copyright 2005 Oxford University Press. Reprinted with permission.

Training resulted in approximately a 0.5 *SD* gain (Schaie, 2005; Willis & Schaie, 1986). Training was most effective for those who declined. Of that group 40% were returned to the level of performance they had experienced 14 years earlier.

Maintenance of Training Gain

The intervention literature is full of reports of immediate gains following brief interventions (pretest–posttest gains). What is of greater concern, however, is whether training gains have any long-lasting effects. This is an area in which only longitudinal studies can provide relevant findings. In the SLS we have now followed trained individuals over 7- and 14-year intervals (Schaie, 2005). Figure 9 shows changes in performance on Inductive Reasoning from initial pretest prior to training to 14 years after training, as compared with a control group that received training on Spatial Orientation. As expected there is further average decline from the first training (M age = 72) to the second pretest (at age 79) and from the second to the third posttest (at age 86). But the trained group even at the oldest age still rose above the initial level, whereas the control group dropped precipitously.

EARLY DETECTION OF RISK OF DEMENTIA

Longitudinal data from the SLS have also been useful in identifying variables that might assist in the early detection of risk for eventual dementia in old age. We pursued this question by expanding our study of community-dwelling persons in which we added a diagnostic neuropsychological battery for participants over age 60 and by collecting data on the ApoE gene to determine its role in cognitive impairment.

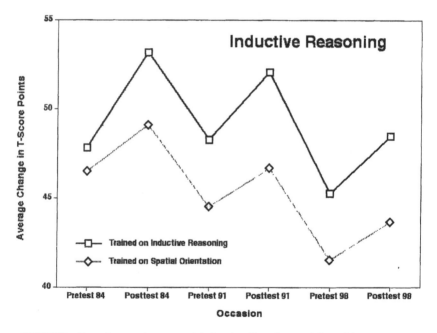

FIGURE 9   Piecewise growth curve models from baseline prior to training to 14-year posttest. From *Developmental Influences on Adult Intelligence: The Seattle Longitudinal Study* (p. 185), by K. W. Schaie, 2005, New York: Oxford University Press. Copyright 2005 Oxford University Press. Reprinted with permission.

Neuropsychology Studies in Community-Dwelling Persons

New questions arise in scientific inquiry that could best be addressed if data were available over time periods. One way of dealing with this problem is to study concurrent data that include the new variables of interest and the variables for which data are available across time. We can thus *postdict*; that is, we can estimate what a longitudinal study participant's score would have been on the data not available for prior occasions. We took this approach to project standard neuropsychological measures into the factor space of our ability by means of extension factor analysis (Dwyer, 1937). By knowing the relationship between the measures that were not available at an earlier time and those that have been given throughout our study, we can then estimate the performance on the unmeasured variables at earlier data points. This procedure allowed us to determine how far back we could have predicted eventual diagnoses of dementia by estimating earlier performance on neuropsychological tests. Our data suggest that it would have been possible, for many persons, to predict the eventual occurrence of dementia at least 14 years prior to the time the actual neuropsychological diagnosis of cognitive impairment occurred (Schaie et al., 2005).

Genetic Studies: The Apoe Gene

The role of the ApoE gene as a risk factor for Alzheimer's disease has been known for some time (Saunders, 2000). In particular, it has been found that presence of the e4 allele is a precursor of dementia. If that is the case, then we should expect excess decrement in cognitive abilities during a portion of the preclinical period. Our longitudinal data allow the requisite analyses, and we find that indeed there is a significantly greater rate of decline over 7 years in individuals with the e4 allele, particularly so for individuals with the e4/2 and e4/4 pairings (Revell & Schaie, 2004; Schaie, 2005).

CONCLUSIONS AND FUTURE DIRECTIONS

In this article I summarized some of the advantages of longitudinal studies of adult development. I provided some of the background and the rationale regarding why cross-sectional methods will not, in most cases, lead to a useful model if questions are to be investigated of intraindividual change, individual aging trajectories, or antecedent–consequent relationships. I also provided examples from the SLS to show how cohort and generation effects cause misleading interpretations of cross-sectional findings. Examples of the use of longitudinal data for estimating rates of age change and generational differences in such rates were given.

Also considered were the utility of longitudinal data in intervention studies and in the prediction cognitive impairment.

Many of the earlier longitudinal studies of adult development were typically based on single markers of the constructs of interest. Current research practice, however, demands that latent constructs should be multiply marked. Hence, we are likely to see increasing emphasis on the study of structural invariance across age and time (cf. Meredith, 1993; Schaie, 2000). Also, in the area of measurement we can expect an increase in multivariate applications of item response theory.

With respect to study design I expect an increase in short-term longitudinal studies in those phases of adulthood where rapid change is likely to occur, whether it be during menopause or in advanced old age. More closely spaced data points would allow the powerful applications of latent growth curve modeling (cf. Rudinger & Rietz, 2001) but would allow the powerful designs derived from the age–cohort–period model (cf. Schaie & Willis, 2002, chap. 5).

As mentioned earlier, longitudinal data are required to study the antecedent–consequent relationships that will eventually lead us from the description of old age to a determination of the mechanism that underlie age changes. Once these mechanisms are identified we will be on the way to developing the interventions necessary to ensure successful aging for most or all of the population.

Finally, I mention the important role of public archives for longitudinal studies of adult development. Even the most persistent investigators cannot follow their study participants from birth to death, and they cannot gather sufficiently large and representative data to permit effective studies of subpopulations. It is, therefore, important that resources be available to document and deposit data from long-term studies so that they can be combined into larger data sets or further explored by other investigators. Examples of public Web sites providing such data access include the National Archives of Computerized Data on Aging Research (http://www.icpsr.umich.edu/NACDA), the public data archive of the SLS (http://geron.psu.edu/sls), and the Murray Center at Radcliffe College (http://www.radcliffe.edu/murray).

REFERENCES

Allison, P. D. (1984). *Event history analysis: Regression for longitudinal event data.* Beverly Hills, CA: Sage.

Arbuckle, Y., Maag, U., Pushkar, D., & Chaikelson, J. S. (1998). Individual differences in trajectory of intellectual development over 45 years of adulthood. *Psychology and Aging, 13,* 663–675.

Baltes, P. B. (1997). On the incomplete architecture of human ontogenesis: Selection, optimization and compensation as foundations of developmental theory. *American Psychologist, 52,* 366–381.

Baltes, P. B., & Baltes, M. M. (1990). Psychological perspectives on successful aging: The model of selective optimization with compensation. In P. B. Baltes & M. M. Baltes (Eds.), *Successful aging: Perspectives from the behavioral sciences* (pp. 1–34). Cambridge, England: Cambridge University Press.

Baltes, P. B., & Lindenberger, U. (1997). Emergence of a powerful connection between sensory and cognitive functions across the adult life span: A new window to the study of cognitive aging. *Psychology and Aging, 12*, 12–21.

Baltes, P. B., & Mayer, K. U. (1999). *The Berlin Aging Study: Aging from 70 to 100.* New York: Cambridge University Press.

Baltes, P. B., & Nesselroade, J. R. (1979). The developmental analysis of individual differences on multiple measures. In J. R. Nesselroade & H. W. Reese (Eds.), *Life-span developmental psychology: Methodological issues* (pp. 1–40). New York: Academic.

Bayley, N., & Oden, M. H. (1955). The maintenance of intellectual ability in gifted adults. *Journal of Gerontology, 10*, 91–107.

Binet, A., & Simon, T. (1905). Méthodes nouvelles pour le diagnostic du niveau intellectuel des anormaux [New methods for the diagnosis of intellectual level of abnormal persons]. *L'Année Psychologique, 11*, 191–199.

Bosworth, H. B., Schaie, K. W., Willis, S. L., & Siegler, I. C. (1999). Age and distance to death in the Seattle Longitudinal Study. *Research on Aging, 21*, 723–738.

Brooks, J., & Weintraub, M. (1976). A history of infant intelligence testing. In M. Lewis (Ed.), *Origins of intelligence* (pp. 19–58). New York: Plenum.

Bryk, A. S., & Raudenbush, S. W. (1987). Application of hierarchical linear models to assessing change. *Psychological Bulletin, 101*, 147–158.

Charness, N., & Schaie, K. W. (Eds.). (2003). *Impact of technology on the aging individual.* New York: Springer.

Cronbach, L. J., & Furby, L. (1970). How should we measure change—or should we? *Psychological Bulletin, 74*, 68–80.

Crystal, S., & Shea, D. (Eds.). (2002). Economic outcomes in later life: Public policy, health and cumulative advantage. *Annual Review of Gerontology and Geriatrics, Vol. 22.*

Czaja, S. J. (2001). Technological change and the older worker. In J. E. Birren & K. W. Schaie (Eds.), *Handbook of the psychology of aging* (5th ed., pp. 547–568). San Diego, CA: Academic.

Dwyer, P. S. (1937). The determination of the factor loadings of a given test from the known factor loadings of other tests. *Psychometrika, 2*, 173–178.

Eichorn, D. H., Clausen, J. A., Haan, N., Honzik, M. P., & Mussen, P. H. (1981). *Present and past in middle life.* New York: Academic.

Flynn, J. R. (1987). Massive gains in 14 nations: What IQ tests really measure. *Psychological Bulletin, 101*, 171–191.

Galton, F. (1869). *Hereditary genius.* London: Macmillan.

Gunning-Dixon, F. M., & Raz, N. (2003). Neuroanatomical correlates of selected executive functions in middle-aged and older adults: A prospective MRI study. *Neuropsychologia, 41*, 1929–1941.

Hall, G. S. (1922). *Senescence, the last half of life.* New York: Appleton.

Harris, C. W. (Ed.). (1963). *Problems in measuring change.* Madison: University of Wisconsin Press.

Hollingsworth, H. L. (1927). *Mental growth and decline: A survey of developmental psychology.* New York: Appleton.

Hultsch, D. F., Hertzog, C., Dixon, R. A., & Small, B. J. (1998). *Memory changes in the aged.* New York: Cambridge University Press.

Jarvik, L. F., Kallman, F. J., & Falek, A. (1962). Intellectual changes in aged twins. *Journal of Gerontology, 17*, 289–294.

Jones, H. E., & Conrad, H. S. (1933). The growth and decline of intelligence: A study of a homogeneous group between the ages of ten and sixty. *Genetic Psychology Monographs, 13*, 223–298.

Lord, F. M. (1956). The measurement of growth. *Educational and Psychological Measurement, 16*, 421–437.

Maitland, S. B., Intrieri, R. C., Schaie, K. W., & Willis, S. L. (2000). Gender differences in cognitive abilities: Invariance of covariance and latent mean structure. *Aging, Neuropsychology and Cognition, 7*, 32–53.

Meredith, W. (1993). Measurement invariance, factor analysis and factorial invariance. *Psychometrika, 58*, 525–543.

Nesselroade, J. R., Stigler, S. M., & Baltes, P. B. (1980). Regression towards the mean and the study of change. *Psychological Bulletin, 88*, 622–637.

Nilsson, L. -G., Bäckman, L., Erngrund, K., Nyberg, L., Adolfsson, R., Bucht, G., Karlsson, S., et al. (1997). The Betula prospective cohort study: Memory, health, and aging. *Aging, Neuropsychology, and Cognition, 4*, 1–32.

Nguyen, H. T. (2000). *Environmental complexity factors: A study of familial similarities and differences.* Unpublished doctoral dissertation, Pennsylvania State University, University Park.

Owens, W. A., Jr. (1953). Age and mental abilities: A longitudinal study. *Genetic Psychology Monographs, 48*, 3–54.

. Owens, W. A., Jr. (1959). Is age kinder to the initially more able? *Journal of Gerontology, 14*, 334–337.

Palmore, E., Busse, E. W., Maddox, G. L., Nowlin, J. B., & Siegler, I. C. (1985). *Normal aging* (Vol. 3). Durham, NC: Duke University Press.

Pew, R. W., & Van Hemel, S. B. (Eds.). (2004). *Technology for adaptive aging.* Washington, DC: National Academy Press.

Plomin, R., & Daniels, D. (1987). Why are two children in the same family so different from each other? *Behavioral and Brain Sciences, 10*, 1–16.

Pressey, S. L., Janney, J. E., & Kuhlen, R. G. (1939). *Life: A psychological survey.* New York: Hayer.

Raz, N., Rodrigue, K. M., & Acker, J. D. (2003). Hypertension and the brain: Vulnerability of the prefrontal regions and executive function. *Behavioral Neuroscience, 117*, 1169–1180.

Reinert, G. (1970). Comparative factor analytic studies of intelligence through the human life span. In L. R. Goulet & P. B. Baltes (Eds.), *Life-span developmental psychology: Research and theory* (pp. 468–485). New York: Academic.

Revell, A. J., & Schaie, K. W. (2004, April). *Domain-specific cognitive deficits associated with ApoE genotype by age group in community-dwelling elderly.* Poster presented at the biennial Cognitive Aging Conference, Atlanta, GA.

Rogosa, D., Brandt, D., & Zimowsky, M. (1982). A growth curve approach to the measurement of change. *Psychological Bulletin, 92*, 726–748.

Rogosa, D., & Willett, J. B. (1985). Understanding correlates of change by modeling individual differences in growth. *Psychometrika, 50*, 203–228.

Rowe, J. W., & Kahn, R. L. (1987). Human aging: Unusual and successful aging. *Science, 237*, 143–149.

Rudinger, G., & Rietz, W. (2001). Structural equation modeling in longitudinal research on aging. In J. E. Birren & K. W. Schaie (Eds.), *Handbook of the psychology of aging* (5th ed., pp. 29–52). San Diego, CA: Academic.

Ryder, N. B. (1965). The cohort as a concept in the study of social changes. *American Sociological Review, 30*, 843–861.

Sanders, A. M. (2000). Apolipoprotein E and Alzheimer disease: An update on genetic and functional analyses. *Journal of Neuropathology and Experimental Neurology, 59*, 751–758.

Schaie, K. W. (1958). Rigidity–flexibility and intelligence: A cross-sectional study of the adult life-span from 20 to 70. *Psychological Monographs, 72*(9, Whole No. 462).

Schaie, K. W. (1959). Cross-sectional methods in the study of psychological aspects of aging. *Journal of Gerontology, 14*, 208–215.

Schaie, K. W. (1965). A general model for the study of developmental problems. *Psychological Bulletin, 64*, 91–107.

Schaie, K. W. (1977). Quasi-experimental designs in the psychology of aging. In J. E. Birren & K. W. Schaie (Eds.), *Handbook of the psychology of aging* (pp. 39–58). New York: Van Nostrand Reinhold.

Schaie, K. W. (1983). What can we learn from the longitudinal study of adult psychological development? In K. W. Schaie (Ed.), *Longitudinal studies of adult psychological development* (pp. 1–19). New York: Guilford.

Schaie, K. W. (1984). Midlife influences upon intellectual functioning in old age. *International Journal of Behavioral Development, 7*, 463–478.

Schaie, K. W. (1985). *Manual for the Schaie–Thurstone Adult Mental Abilities Test (STAMAT)*. Palo Alto, CA: Consulting Psychologists Press.

Schaie, K. W. (1989). The hazards of cognitive aging. *Gerontologist, 29*, 484–493.

Schaie, K. W. (1996). *Intellectual development in adulthood: The Seattle Longitudinal Study*. New York: Cambridge University Press.

Schaie, K. W. (2000). Longitudinal and related methodological issues in the Swedish Twin Registry. In B. Smedby, I. Lundberg, & T. I. A. Sørensen (Eds.), *Scientific evaluation of the Swedish Twin Registry* (pp. 62–74). Stockholm, Sweden: Swedish Council for Planning and Coordination of Research.

Schaie, K. W. (2005). *Developmental influences on adult intelligence: The Seattle Longitudinal Study*. New York: Oxford University Press.

Schaie, K. W., Caskie, G. I. L., Revell, A. J., Willis, S. L., Kaszniak, A. W., & Teri, L. (2005). Extending neuropsychological assessment into the Primary Mental Ability factor space. *Aging, Neuropsychology and Cognition, 12*.

Schaie, K. W., & Hofer, S. M. (2001). Longitudinal studies in research on aging. In J. E. Birren & K. W. Schaie (Eds.), *Handbook of the psychology of aging* (5th ed., pp. 55–77). San Diego, CA: Academic.

Schaie, K. W., Maitland, S. B., Willis, S. L., & Intrieri, R. L. (1998). Longitudinal invariance of adult psychometric ability factor structures across seven years. *Psychology and Aging, 13*, 8–20.

Schaie, K. W., Plomin, R., Willis, S. L., Gruber-Baldini, A., & Dutta, R. (1992). Natural cohorts: Family similarity in adult cognition. In T. Sonderegger (Ed.), *Psychology and aging: Nebraska Symposium on Motivation, 1991* (pp. 205–243). Lincoln, NE: University of Nebraska Press.

Schaie, K. W., Plomin, R., Willis, S. L., Gruber-Baldini, A. L., Dutta, R., & Bayen, U. (1993). Family similarity in adult intellectual development. In J. J. F. Schroots (Ed.), *Aging, health and competence: The next generation of longitudinal research* (pp. 183–198). Amsterdam: Elsevier.

Schaie, K. W., & Schooler, C. E. (Eds.). (1998). *Impact of the work place on older persons*. New York: Springer.

Schaie, K. W., & Willis, S. L. (2002). *Adult development and aging*. Upper Saddle River, NJ: Prentice-Hall.

Schaie, K. W., Willis, S. L., & Caskie, G. I. L. (2004). The Seattle Longitudinal Study: Relation between personality and cognition. *Aging, Neuropsychology and Cognition, 11*, 304–324.

Schaie, K. W., & Zuo, Y. L. (2001). Family environments and adult cognitive functioning. In R. L. Sternberg & E. Grigorenko (Eds.), *Context of intellectual development* (pp. 337–361). Mahwah, NJ: Lawrence Erlbaum Associates, Inc.

Singer, J. D., & Willett, J. B. (1991). Modeling the days of our lives: Using survival analysis when designing and analyzing longitudinal studies of duration and the time of events. *Psychological Bulletin, 110*, 268–290.

Solomon, D. H. (1999). The role of aging processes in age-dependent diseases. In V. L. Bengtson & K. W. Schaie (Eds.), *Handbook of theories of aging* (pp. 133–152). New York: Springer.

Sörbom, D., & Jöreskog, K. G. (1978). *Confirmatory factor analysis with model modification*. Chicago: International Educational Services.

Staudinger, U. M., Maciel, A. G., Smith J., & Baltes, P. B. (1998). What predicts wisdom-related performance? A first look at personality, intelligence, and facilitative experiential contexts. *European Journal of Personality, 12*, 1–17.

Sternberg, R. J., & Lubart, T. I. (2001). Wisdom and creativity. In J. E. Birren & K. W. Schaie (Eds.), *Handbook of the psychology of aging* (5th ed., pp. 500–522). San Diego, CA: Academic.

Terman, L. M. (1916). *The measurement of intelligence.* Boston: Houghton.

Thorndike, E. L. (1924). The influence of chance imperfections of measures upon the relation of initial scores to gains or loss. *Journal of Experimental Psychology, 7,* 225–232.

Thurstone, L. L. (1947). *Multiple factor analysis.* Chicago: University of Chicago Press.

Thurstone, L. L., & Thurstone, T. G. (1949). *Examiner manual for the SRA Primary Mental Abilities Test.* Chicago: Science Research Associates.

Tucker, L. R. (1958). Determination of parameters of a functional relation by factor analysis. *Psychometrika, 23,* 19–23.

Wechsler, D. (1939). *The measurement of adult intelligence.* Baltimore: Williams & Wilkins.

Willett, J. B. (1989). Some results on reliability for the longitudinal measurement of change: Implications for the design of studies of individual growth. *Educational and Psychological Measurement, 49,* 587–601.

Willett, J. B., & Sayer, A. G. (1994). Using covariance structure analysis to detect correlations and predictors of individual change over time. *Psychological Bulletin, 116,* 363–381.

Willis, S. L. (2001). Methodological issues in behavioral intervention research with the elderly. In J. E. Birren & K. W. Schaie (Eds.), *Handbook of the psychology of aging* (5th ed., pp. 78–108). San Diego, CA: Academic.

Willis, S. L., & Dubin, S. (Eds.). (1990). *Maintaining professional competence.* San Francisco: Jossey-Bass.

Willis, S. L., & Reid, J. E. (Eds.). (1999). *Life in the middle: Psychological and social development in middle age.* San Diego, CA: Academic.

Willis, S. L., & Schaie, K. W. (1986). Training the elderly on the ability factors of spatial orientation and inductive reasoning. *Psychology and Aging, 1,* 239–247.

Wohlwill, J. (1973). *The study of behavioral development.* New York: Academic.

Yerkes, R. M. (1921). Psychological examining in the United States Army. *Memoirs of the National Academy of Sciences, 15,* 1–890.

*For Product Safety Concerns and Information please contact
our EU representative GPSR@taylorandfrancis.com Taylor & Francis
Verlag GmbH, Kaufingerstraße 24, 80331 München, Germany*

T - #0164 - 270225 - C0 - 229/152/3 - PB - 9780805894233 - Gloss Lamination